MAKING TRACKS

MAKING TRACKS

Atlantic Records and the Growth
of a Multi-Billion-Dollar Industry

CHARLIE GILLETT

SOUVENIR PRESS

This British Edition published 1988 by
Souvenir Press Ltd., 43 Great Russell Street, London WC1B 3PA

ISBN 0 285 62831 3

Printed and bound in Great Britain by
Biddles Ltd., Guildford and King's Lynn

CONTENTS

MAKING TRACKS

FOREWORD:
THEY CHANGED OUR
CHARTS AROUND

This book is about songs and money—the music business. Songs affect and involve us deeply, yet we hardly know how. Are we servants or masters of the men who sell us records?

Up until the mid-1950s the owners of small record companies, known in the trade as "independents," based their operations on the assumption or hope that they would sometimes sell 100,000 copies of a record. But during the mid-fifties. several of these companies found that they could sell ten times more: a million. Just because they happened to have a singer who sang what the disc jockeys were calling "rock 'n' roll."

This rock 'n' roll music was the center of my adolescent attention (along with sport and fantasies of sex), but for these businessmen it was a product which carried them to the top of their industry and put them alongside the

60-year-old giants, CBS and RCA. There were five small companies in particular which consistently put out magically effective records: Sun, Specialty, Chess, Imperial, and Atlantic. Sun had early Elvis, Jerry Lee Lewis, Carl Perkins, and Johnny Cash; Specialty had Little Richard; Chess had Chuck Berry and Bo Diddley; Imperial had Fats Domino; and Atlantic had Clyde McPhatter, LaVern Baker, Joe Turner, Ray Charles, and the Coasters.

As a 15-year-old British record buyer in 1957, I wasn't aware of these different labels. In Great Britain most of the independent American companies were licensed to British Decca, who put all the stuff out on the London label. I bought records by Chuck Berry, Fats Domino, and Little Richard, but nothing from the Atlantic singers: either they sounded strange and unattractive at the time, like Clyde McPhatter, or they weren't being played at all on British radio.

I didn't hear Atlantic's classic records until 1963, when I bought a compilation LP called *Rock and Roll Forever, Volume One.* The sleeve notes on the album said that these recordings were the original versions of well-known songs by other performers. I already knew the "cover" version of several of these songs: "Shake, Rattle, and Roll," "Money Honey," "Tweedle Dee," "I Got A Woman," and "One Mint Julep." Listening to the originals was a revelation.

In every case the "original" sounded much better than the copies I had heard over the radio. I felt outraged and cheated by a system which had kept these hidden from me. The piano introduction to Joe Turner's "Shake, Rattle, and Roll" was the perfect setup for Joe's opening, shouted command: "Get out of that bed, and wash you face and hands." Get out of bed? Bill Haley had never sung that line. A world opened up, in which recorded songs were representations of everyday scenes in an adult life, not teenage bubblegum fantasies. Clyde McPhatter's interpretation of "Money Honey," the fourth cut on the album, confirmed this "realistic" approach to song lyrics: "Well the landlord rang my front door bell. . . ."

LaVern Baker's "Tweedle Dee" was lyrically inane, but there was a suggestive tone in her voice which made even nonsense words hold all kinds of promises. The track after "Tweedle Dee" was "One Mint Julep" by the Clovers. Once again, a real situation which has the singer getting himself drunk, a girl into trouble, and them both into marriage: "I'm through flirtin' and drinkin' whiskey, I got six extra children from gettin' frisky." All this, and I was only half-way through side one; I still had three tracks to go: Ray Charles as a deadpan comedian in "It Should've Been Me," Ruth Brown and T-Bone Walker, each relaxed and mellow in their respective renditions of "5-10-15 Hours" and "T-Bone Shuffle." The sax solos on these last two tracks were tiny masterpieces in the art of saying everything in less than thirty seconds, and apparently without any effort at all.

The combination of very strong content, accurate yet still improvised singing, and imaginative accompaniments made these tracks stand up to more repeated plays than most rock 'n' roll LPs, and planted the seeds of a curiosity and affection for music of the mid-fifties and its singers, writers, and producers. This curiosity grew first into a general history of the music, *The Sound of the City,* and now into this account of Atlantic records. I had tried to describe the stylistic developments of the "rock 'n' roll revolution," the only revolution in the 80-year-old history of the American record industry. Now, I wanted to meet some of the people who had engineered that revolution, the producers and musicians, and the men who owned the labels.

One reason for choosing Atlantic rather than any of

the other independent record companies is that Atlantic is still thriving under essentially the same management that founded and developed it. None of the other "independents" are in a similar situation. Specialty's founder Art Rupe still runs his company, but principally to market compilation LPs of material recorded in the forties and fifties. Lew Chudd of Imperial and Sam Phillips of Sun both sold their catalogues to other record companies, and Leonard Chess died a couple of years ago. Meanwhile, Atlantic has expanded so much that it can no longer be called an independent. In the month that I was carrying out the bulk of interviews for this book, April 1971, the company sold ten million dollars' worth of records. Throughout 1971–72 Atlantic often had ten 45s in *Billboard*'s Hot 100, has always had at least ten albums in the list of 100 Bestselling LPs, and for a couple of weeks in the summer of 1972 had six albums in the top 10: *Exile On Main Street* by the Rolling Stones (on the Stones' label which is distributed by Atlantic); two albums by Roberta Flack (one solo and the other with Donny Hathaway); *Manassas* by Stephen Stills; *The History of Eric Clapton*; and an album by David Crosby and Graham Nash. Only CBS-Epic, with much larger financial resources, more releases, and a huge easy listening catalogue closely tied into TV shows on its own network, can rival Atlantic's sales over the past three years.

There is an aura about Atlantic, which can be felt as soon as the outsider puts his foot on the edge of the music business. During the time I've been working as a freelance music journalist in Britain, I've continually noticed how performers, who invariably criticize their record companies, would have some positive comment to make about Atlantic. In particular, I was impressed by the strong loyalty toward Atlantic of Clyde McPhatter and Ben E. (Benny) King, former lead singers for the Drifters, who each launched a solo career with Atlantic but drifted into semi-obscurity after a few years.

Clyde McPhatter recorded for Atlantic for seven years, first with the Drifters and then on his own, but after making the top 10 in 1959 with "A Lover's Question" he switched to MGM. "I didn't want to leave Atlantic," he recalled with remorse ten years later. "I enjoyed working there. Ahmet Ertegun was a marvelous man. But my manager, Irving Feld, disagreed with Ahmet about something, and he signed me up to MGM. Nothing much happened in a year, and we moved to Mercury. I had some hits there, but I would still rather have stayed at Atlantic."

Desperate for a stable career, Clyde moved to Britain in 1968 and stayed for a couple of years. Nobody noticed. He went back to the States, made an album for Decca which sank without trace, and early in 1972 he called up Jerry Wexler, wanting to come back to Atlantic to make a record. Jerry sent him some money, but wouldn't cut a record with him. Atlantic wasn't into charity recordings. A few months later, Clyde was dead.

Ben E. King's case was slightly different. After six years of consistent hits, first with the Drifters and then on his own, he stayed with the company for three more years, making records which sold poorly in an era dominated by harder-voiced "soul" singers like Otis Redding and Wilson Pickett. According to Benny, he left of his own accord, still on friendly terms with Atlantic. "They're very beautiful, very honest, very true people. You couldn't find better people to be with. They've stayed with an artist when he's going down, down, and they stayed with me. I said to myself, I'll give myself one more record, and if that don't happen, I'll leave, to keep myself from feeling that I'm sinking. I didn't want a recording session that was being held because they felt, well, this is Benny and he's been here eleven years so we'll give him one."

Celebrating Atlantic's 25th birthday in Paris.
Left to right: Nesuhi Ertegun, Ahmet Ertegun
and Jerry Wexler.

Not only was Atlantic known for treating its artists sympathetically, but it was above all others the label that got a *clean* sound, able to filter a tight sound out of a rough group without sacrificing spontaneity. Mac Rebennack, a New Orleans song writer and session musician long before he adopted the stage persona of Dr. John the Night Tripper, bears witness to Atlantic's skill in transforming the casual products of New Orleans recording sessions into finished products: "They changed our charts around, the way their records was put together. You could hear what every instrument was playing, real clear, and everybody was in tune. Man, that was something else." Atlantic was also known for paying royalty checks in those early days of rock 'n' roll, a time when many other companies regularly held pirate recording sessions, paid musicians under the union rates, and rarely considered coughing up royalties.

Finally, Atlantic is a record company with character—not a faceless corporation. It is known for the people who run it. Ahmet Ertegun, the co-founder and president of Atlantic and an inveterate prankster, has a public personality as mysterious and evocative as his name. And Jerry Wexler, the vice-president of the company who joined a few years after its founding, is mentioned by so many performers with a tone of affection, admiration, and respect, that he has become one of the few record company executives and studio producers who is known to the casual record buyer.

Of all the record companies, Atlantic seemed the most satisfying to write about. There was, for one thing, Jerry Wexler's own writing: liner notes mostly, and a few articles for *Billboard.* His long description of Ray Charles' musical career on the two-volume set *The Ray Charles.Story* was some of the most interesting sleeve copy I had ever read. And the *Billboard* article, "What It Is, Is Swamp Music," expressed with wit and love from first hand some of the feelings that I had been struggling to articulate four thousand miles away, about Joe South, Tony Joe White, and a new "Southern Sound" that I could see developing. I made it a condition of writing the book that I would spend some time with Jerry Wexler.

When I first met him at the Miami Airport in April 1971, Jerry's first concern was whether I was okay for financing the book. If I was tight, he could loan me $5,000, to be repaid when I had it to spare—it would be no problem, so long as Atlantic's name was on the front jacket somewhere. As we drove to his house in a battered old open car, the wind carrying our words away, I was pleased and baffled at what he was offering. But then how could

I be sure I would not be tied down by the money in some way. He guessed my thoughts. "No strings, no ties. You still write what you want to write. And if you find there's no book there after all, no sweat."

Still I said no, and he didn't raise the question again. He did say again, though, that it didn't matter if no book came out of my project. I wondered, and wonder, why did he think there might be no story there?

ONE:
I HAD TROUBLE WITH
MY PARTNERS

I arrived in New York on a Saturday in April 1971 to research a book on the record business, in particular, Atlantic Records. How was it that of all the independent New York record companies, Atlantic was the one to survive and grow?

Most of the other companies that started in the late forties and early fifties had "folded" during the early sixties, and although their founders were probably working somewhere on the fringe of the record business, I had no means of tracing them. But I had read a few magazine articles which referred to a Harlem record store owner called Bobby Robinson, who had put out records on a succession of labels since 1953, some of which were hits. Wilbert Harrison's "Kansas City," a number 1 hit in 1959, was on Bobby's Fury label. Why hadn't he consolidated the income from that hit and others, and built himself a solid record company? It seemed strange that there was no big black-owned, Harlem-based record company; had Atlantic's midtown operation prospered partly through the default of Harlem's businessmen? I had read somewhere that during the early days of Atlantic, its inexperienced founders Ahmet Ertegun and Herb Abramson used to take demonstration records uptown for Bobby Robinson to hear. If they sounded commercial to him, they would release them.

On Sunday, I took the subway up to 125th Street, hoping to find Bobby's store, but leaving my recorder and camera behind. I didn't want anyone to mistake me for a tourist. One of the magazine articles had described Bobby's store as being a block away from the Apollo, and sure enough, there was a little store the size of a bathroom, with a speaker blasting onto the sidewalk. Inside, a couple of guys stood behind the counter, selling records. One of them, small, neatly-dressed, watching me, was Bobby. Seeing how busy he was, I asked if I could come back during the week to interview him, fixed a provisional time, and went out to stand next to the speaker on the sidewalk. Although I had heard and read the rumors that Harlem was a dangerous place for white people to hang out, I retained a stubborn faith that, if I made it obvious that I loved the music, I'd be all right.

So I stood there on the sidewalk, taking in a Roy C. record that was being played over and over again. I must have had my eyes closed, because out of nowhere I suddenly heard a voice saying, "I want a drink." I looked at a girl, 15 or 16 years old, scrawny, not my type even if I had been out to pick somebody up. Here I'd just come for the music, and I was being accosted. What would I do now, if a black guy came up to me like the man in Lou Reed's song: "Hey white boy, what you doin' uptown? Hey white boy, you chasin' our women around?"

"What do you want me to do about it?" I asked cautiously,

expecting some suggestion like we go to the nearest bar. "Give me the money to go and buy a soda over there," she said, pointing to a soda fountain on the opposite corner of the intersection. I pulled out a dollar and asked her to get me one too. Minutes later, she came back with two cans and some change, and left me feeling confused and ashamed at my suspicions.

Next door to Bobby's was a hot dog store. I went inside and ordered one, for here. Looking out the window as I ate it, seeing nothing in particular, I became aware that a conversation between two people near me was intended for me to hear. I turned so that I was almost looking at one of them, registered that they were two young guys, 17 or 18 years old, one of whom was saying, "So what do you think of it, up here?" And in a voice that took an unaccountably long time to make a sound, I said, "Fine, yeah, it's great." And the kid said "Right on," and walked out with his friend.

Encouraged, and less worried about how conspicuous I looked, I took a little tour of 125th, winding up at the Apollo. I went inside to ask for the stage manager, who I hoped might tell me something about Atlantic and the people who recorded for the Atlantic label. And perhaps he would be able to explain why so few black singers sustain their careers, at least compared to country singers, who retain their appeal for spans of twenty years or more.

The Apollo's stage manager was a former tap dancer—"hoofer," he called it—named Honi Coles. By all accounts Honi rivaled Fred Astaire for speed and grace. He did have an explanation for the short-lived careers of black singers: their lack of concern for stagecraft. Over the years Honi has stood by in despair as he witnessed the decay of the art of presenting an act on stage; either it has been destroyed by the extravagant provocations of Jackie Wilson, James Brown, and Wilson Pickett, or else simply spurned by singers like Marvin Gaye and Tyrone Davis who seem to expect to hold an audience's attention without making any effort to involve them beyond just singing.

"We tried to persuade Jackie Wilson to get rid of his dirty act, to sing for the family audience we have here. He should have taken lessons at an acting school on how to project himself, to step into any role. But he didn't survive his era. It's the tragedy of show business. Wilson Pickett, though, has acquired finesse. He used to be dirty, but now he thinks about the whole audience."

He didn't survive his era: that was a way of expressing the major problem in a singer's career that I had never heard before. "Era" meant the period of having hit singles. To survive it meant to appeal to a live audience, regardless of recent record sales. Billy Eckstine has survived his era. Clyde McPhatter did not, and the vast majority of black singers and vocal groups did not. I had always believed that the record companies were largely responsible for the brevity of most careers, because they treated the performers so badly that there was little incentive to keep trying. But most of what I knew about record companies had been picked up from interviews in the music press with the performers, who rarely had much good to say about the way their companies treated them. Here was Honi suggesting that the performers lacked the talent or versatility to hold their audiences.

I left the Apollo and went back to stand outside Bobby Robinson's store. After a while Bobby came out to stand beside me. He pointed across the road. "See those windows on the first floor, that was our office when we had Fury. Come around the corner, and I'll show you where I'm going to expand the store." We had to step over a couple of winos in a doorway. After we'd passed them, Bobby indicated one of them and said: "See the one on the left, he's a real good blues singer. I've recorded an album with him, but I haven't figured out what kind of style to release it in, downhome acoustic, or more modern electric."

Back in the store, we listened to some of the tracks on the demo LP Bobby had made from the blues singer's sessions, unremarkable but not bad. "That's my music, the blues," Bobby said as his assistant took off the LP and replaced it with a current soul 45. Bobby picked up a list that the assistant had been making up during the afternoon, a list of titles that the store was running short of. Bobby had to go to a distributor to pick up some replacements, and I tagged along.

In the taxi, I asked Bobby why so many of his labels had folded. "I had trouble with my partners." Since I was enjoying the ride, I didn't press him for details, but asked instead how he got started. "I grew up in South Carolina, and came to New York in 1937 when I was 18. I just scuffled around for a long time, had a shoeshine parlor for a while, and a record store, and I formed my first label in 1953, Red Robin. I knew what people were buying from what people asked for in the store, so I knew I could sell some kinds of blues, and vocal groups."

Over the years his labels had a number of hits, but most of Bobby's memories were of the singers and records he missed: of how Frankie Lymon and the Teenagers rehearsed in his store and then signed with Roulette, or of the tape that Ike Turner sent while Bobby was out of town, or the Otis Redding record he rejected. "Yeah, in sixty or sixty-one I had this record sent to me from a little company in Georgia, Otis Redding singing "Shout Bamalama" on the Confederate label. And I thought, what's this, you know, it didn't sound too good to me from the start, having a label name like that, with the confederate flag on it and all. But I put the record on, and it was an imitation of Little Richard. This was when Richard was in his gospel phase, and that sound was as dead as could be, so I didn't follow it up at all. About a year later, I was listening to the radio, and this great slow blues came on, 'These Arms Of Mine,' and I thought, what a great singer he is. I couldn't believe it when the disc jockey said it was Otis Redding. I shouted, why didn't you send me that one?"

At the distributors' we went around a stack of records and picked up more than 100 45s, a few LPs, and some cartridges, while Bobby carried on bantering conversations with the assistants and other customers. He was more serious with a stocky man who was also buying a lot of records, a man Bobby identified outside as his brother Danny, a partner in some of Bobby's labels, and co-owner of the publishing company, Bob-Dan Music.

Recording both locally in New York and along the Eastern Seaboard of the Carolinas, the Robinson brothers documented an interesting collection of rhythm and blues artists, most of whom supplied their own material and musical arrangements. Perhaps because they were easiest to record, vocal groups dominated the rosters of the Robinsons' various labels, the most successful being the Channels with "The Closer You Are" (on Whirlin' Disc), the Charts with "Deserie" (on Everlast), and Gladys Knight and the Pips with "Every Beat of My Heart" (on Fury). Among their other hits were "The Sky Is Crying" (on Fire) and "It Hurts Me Too" (on Enjoy) by singer/guitarist Elmore James, and "Soul Twist" (on Enjoy) by session saxman King Curtis.

Back at the store, Bobby handed the new records over to his assistant, who had already started a new list of 45s he was running short on. I asked how long the stock we had just brought in would last. To the end of the week? "No, most of them will be gone by the time we close tonight." I began to see the logic of the shop, how Bobby could keep on top of the rapidly changing, unpredictable taste of the R and B audience. He had slots for about

100 different 45 titles along the wall behind the counter: as each pile was reduced to the last two or three copies, and if people were still asking for it, more copies were picked up from the distributor, which is collectively owned by several Harlem record stores. It was one of the most efficient operations I'd ever seen. So why couldn't Bobby have translated this efficiency into his handling of the record business? I asked about Wilbert Harrison's "Kansas City."

Wilbert Harrison was a one-man band who had been with Savoy, an independent company based in Newark, since 1954. In March 1959, Wilbert told Bobby that his contract with Savoy was over, and that he had a song which had been going down well in his live act for five years, a reworking of Little Willie Littlefield's 1952 record, "K. C. Lovin'," which Wilbert had retitled "Kansas City." With a couple of session musicians, little rehearsal, and less than thirty minutes' studio time, Wilbert cut "Kansas City" and a B side. "It cost me forty dollars," Bobby remembered, "and it sold well over a million copies."

"Kansas City" succeeded despite almost every obstacle that can halt a record's progress. Before pressing a substantial number of copies of the record, Bobby made twelve one-sided demo "dubs." He left these with dee jays in various cities while he went off on a promotion trip for another record he had high hopes for ("My Love Will Never Die" by the Channels). By the time he was back in New York and went to the office, after almost two weeks on the road to Cleveland, Detroit, Chicago, New Orleans, and Atlanta, he couldn't open the door.

"There was all this resistance, and I was wondering, what is this? I finally got the door open, and I was knee-deep in telegrams. And they were all about the same thing, "Kansas City." I had no idea, but the record had broken wide open everywhere, people were calling the radio stations and distributors, but nobody had any copies to sell,

I hadn't pressed any. A disc jockey in Cleveland had taped the record off the air, and had done a note-for-note copy with a local white kid called Rocky Olson, which he sent to Leonard Chess in Chicago, who had put it on the market already. I'd been covered, and I didn't have my own record out yet!"

Al Bennett of Liberty and Randy Wood of Dot Records both wanted to license the Wilbert Harrison version of the song, and so did George Goldner of Gone and End, who said he had made a cover version of the song which he wouldn't release if he could have the Harrison version for his label.

But Bobby chose to go it alone. And although there were simultaneous hit versions of the song on Chess, Federal (by Hank Ballard and the Midnighters), and Specialty (by Little Richard), Wilbert Harrison on Fury made number 1. But it was hardly worth it, because as soon as the Harrison record started to sell, Herman Lubinsky of Savoy Records filed a suit claiming all the money that was accruing to Fury. Although Savoy issued only four records by Wilbert in four years, and although Herman had told Wilbert not to bother to come back to make any more, the contract was in fact not due to expire until August, six months after the "Kansas City" session. Lubinsky sued Fury for anything between $150,000 and $250,000, but settled for the more modest sum of $13,500. Meanwhile Armo, the publishers who represented Leiber and Stoller's composition, "K. C. Lovin'," also filed a suit against Fury for failing to notify the publishers of the impending recording of their song.

It seemed I had found out why Bobby Robinson never made it as a major record man, and why Atlantic had survived. While Bobby took insufficient care as to whom he recorded and whose songs he used, I thought Atlantic must have operated with more forethought and calculation. But that was before I met Ahmet Ertegun, Herb Abramson, and Jerry Wexler, none of whom made any claims to be great organization men.

TWO:
HOW TO MAKE A BUCK

I

Ahmet Ertegun decided to go into the record business in 1947. He didn't know the first thing about making records, still less about selling them, and two previous shots at starting companies had been complete, if inconspicuous, failures. But Ahmet had evolved a few principles by which he intended to live, which had crystalized when his father, the Turkish ambassador to Washington, died in 1944. "I didn't want to go in the army, and I didn't want to work." Studying philosophy and making records seemed to meet his terms perfectly.

Philosophy he was qualified for. He had been one of the top students in his class at St. John's College, so it was an easy step to the postgraduate course at Georgetown University in Washington. And if fanatical enthusiasm counted for anything, it wasn't such a big jump for him to start making records either. With his elder brother Nesuhi, Ahmet had collected more than 15,000 jazz and blues 78s, some of them bought new but a lot more found for five or ten cents on door-to-door rounds of black neighborhoods in Washington or nearby Maryland and Virginia. In addition, Ahmet had helped his brother, and a friend from New York named Herb Abramson, stage jazz concerts in Washington, so he knew several of the most famous musicians personally—Sidney Bechet, Charlie Parker, Lester Young. He'd read the specialist magazines, met many collectors, and could tell you the lineup on all Louis Armstrong's records.

When Ahmet's father died, his mother went back to Turkey, and Nesuhi went to live on the West Coast. Ahmet had to move to a smaller apartment, where there was no room for 15,000 78s. The brothers auctioned them off, getting from five to twenty-five dollars for records that had often cost them a nickel or a dime. The money was a useful supplement to Ahmet's allowance, but eventually ran out.

Ahmet began to think about ways of making a living that didn't contravene his principles. "Eventually I came around to thinking about running a record label myself. I figured I could do it by working on it one day a week, putting out just a few records. I thought that if one out of ten shops in America were to buy just one of my records, I could make some money. That was my projection, right? I had no idea about how records were pressed, who distributed them, what happened. It just never occured to me, how a record came to be in a shop."

The problem of distribution never arose the first time. A friend put up some money to do a session with the Boyd Raeburn jazz band, nominally supervised by Ahmet. But the musical arrangements were by Johnny Richards;

the recording was done by the engineer; Ahmet simply hung around trying to work out what everybody else was doing. No record was ever pressed, no label named.

The second time Ahmet got together with Herb Abramson, and a couple of records were actually issued, because Herb had a solid background as a record producer. But although records did get out to the stores on labels named Quality and Jubilee, the company never got off the ground. Partly because Ahmet miscalculated the life style of the independent record company man: "I thought the way to get into the music business was to make a good impression. So when I went to New York, I hired a suite at the Ritz, which was probably the best hotel in the city. But although I spent all the money I had, I wasn't getting anywhere. After a couple of months, I had had a very good time, but I hadn't come close to making a record.

"So I decided I'd better get back with Herb and really get down to putting a company into action. I went back to Washington and asked my dentist to lend me ten thousand dollars. I was asking him to take a chance on somebody who had never done a day's work in his life, who had made two abortive attempts at starting a record company. But he was a gambler. And it turned out to be one of the best investments ever made. He didn't even have to put up the full ten thousand, because by the time he came to put up the last part, he was already getting money back from what we were making.

"I moved in with Herb and his wife Miriam, who had an inexpensive flat in the Village where I used to sleep on the couch. By now I was worrying about another failure. And I must say that Herb knew a lot about the record business and I knew next to nothing. Except that I had a sense of what might sell. Which Herb had too."

Herb Abramson had been a collector of jazz and blues

records since his high school days in Brooklyn, and during the war promoted jazz concerts, some of them in association with the Ertegun brothers in Washington, and some by himself in New York. "At that time, the musicians' union scale for concerts was similar to the rate for dances, so you could get an allstar ten-piece band for the same basic minimum as an ordinary dance band. Of course we would also guarantee them a percentage of the gate, but it meant we could get them for a basic two hundred and fifty dollars—twenty-five dollars per man." Organizing these concerts, Herb chose musicians that he liked, rather than those who were used to playing together, and it subsequently became almost a trademark of his to record unusual combinations of styles.

Together, in 1947, Herb and Ahmet launched Atlantic Records, Herb as president, Ahmet as vice-president.

II

From the beginning, Atlantic had a distinctly different image from most other "indie" record firms. The easygoing nature of the dentist who lent Ahmet the money to start the venture, Dr. Sabit, was important. Sabit undoubtedly hoped not to lose money, but to see some profit. But he was not the kind of man to put pressure on Ahmet to "deliver," or to insist that Atlantic make a star out of his secretary, or to threaten all kinds of horror if his four best friends weren't made directors of the firm, or at least salesmen for it. So most of the decisions Herb and Ahmet took were based on their own judgment, and they didn't have to cheat their performers in order to make all the payoffs that were often expected of their indie rivals.

Herb and Ahmet gained a reputation for being more honest than their street-educated competitors, and as much as anything else that reputation, the good image, was the foundation that the company's success was built on; it meant that many talented performers signed long-term contracts with Atlantic because they believed the promise that royalties would be paid.

Herb Abramson had seen at close quarters how other kinds of record companies operated in 1946, when he acted as a part-time record producer for National Records, while attending New York University, College of Dentistry. National Records was formed shortly after the end of the war by Al Green, with Jerry Blaine as sales manager. According to Herb, "Al Green got into the record business through the paint business." Green was an operator who joined the painters' union and formed his own paint company with the aid of "some of the boys." During the war one of his employees worked out a formula to make varnish a different way; somebody pointed out that there was a shortage of shellac for making records, and that perhaps this formula would work for records as well. "So Al had a few biscuits pressed out of this new stuff and they sounded like they were made out of a mixture of gravel and manure but they did work, you could hear the music. So Al started selling a lot of these biscuits to the newly emerging independent record companies, until he began to realize the amount of money that was to be made in the record business. So, ever a shrewd guy, Al bought a lot of old presses from the Gennett Company in Richmond, Indiana, that hadn't been used since before the depression, and with parts from some other presses—just as old—he assembled a plant in Phillipsburg, New Jersey, held together with baling wire, and started National Records.

"Al Green was a guy who knew and cared nothing about music, a crude, tough man, one of the three grand old men of the indie record business—along with Herman Lubinsky of Savoy, and Sidney Nathan of King—rough,

*Herb Abramson (left) with Clyde McPhatter,
working on the session that produced Clyde's hit,
"Seven Days."*

ignorant guys who knew how to make a buck." Since Al
couldn't produce his own records, he needed somebody
to look after the creative side, and Herb was his man.

"Al had a lady doing his A and R work at the beginning,
but she was more interested in classical music than popular
music, and I heard from a collector friend that there was
a job open, applied for it, and got it.

"Because of my interest in jazz, the first people I signed
up were in that field, Pete Johnson and Joe Turner. And
it happened that the people I was interested in turned

out to have a wider appeal. There was a hit by the Earl Hines Orchestra at that time, 'Jelly Jelly,' with Billy Eckstine singing on it. So when I read that Billy was going to start his own orchestra, I ran down to his booking agency, Bill Shaw, to try to make a deal for him to record for National. Of course he wanted to know why I thought Billy Eckstine should sign with a new little firm like National, and wanted an advance of two thousand dollars a session. A session in those days was four sides, so this was five hundred dollars a side, a lot for those days but I thought it was worth it, and went back to ask Al if he would agree to those terms. He did.

"I had an old record by Russ Colombo in my collection, 'Prisoner Of Love,' which I thought would suit Billy's voice. We recorded it and had a very big hit, and followed it up with another, 'Cottage For Sale.'

"I also signed up the Ravens, and groomed them to become the second Ink Spots. They had a great bass in Jimmy Ricks, and also a very fine high tenor, Maithe Marshall; Ben Bart at the Universal Attractions booking agency had put them together, and I heard them during their first week at the Apollo.

"One of the biggest hits I had there was with Dusty Fletcher, the black comedian. He had a stage routine built around the phrase, 'Open The Door, Richard,' and a West Coast bandleader, Jack McVae, recorded a song with that title. So I had the idea of getting Dusty to do it; I had a hard time finding him, but finally tracked him down in a hotel room in South Carolina and persuaded him to make a record. He'd never done one before and didn't think he should, but eventually agreed. And we got a big hit."

With this experience tucked under his belt, Herb left Al Green with the idea of doing something by himself. "I decided to go out on my own after three years with

National. I'd noticed that there was a division in the Negro audience between gospel and jazz, so I started the Jubilee label for gospel and Quality for jazz. Quality was taken from the name of Max Silverman's record shop in Washington, where Ahmet had spent many hours listening to records. Max was a good friend, who helped whenever he could. I was going to go into partnership with Ahmet, but that fell through and I continued with Jubilee on my own and later formed a partnership with Jerry Blaine in New York, but after I'd done a record on each label—one of them was by the gospel singer Ernestine Washington, backed up by Bunk Johnson's jazz band— Jerry started putting out Jewish comedy records on Jubilee which sold very well but which didn't interest me. So I asked him to buy me out and soon after went into partnership with Ahmet in Atlantic Records. If you look at the labels, you'll see that the design on the Atlantic label, with the big capital A reaching down the left hand side of the label, is the same as that on the Jubilee and Quality labels."

Though in very different positions in 1971, both Ahmet Ertegun and Herb Abramson remember those early years fondly and in some detail, even if there seems to be some confusion over exactly which of them did what.

III

Given the extent to which the record business now comprises either large and complex institutions, or smaller firms with underworld connections, the story of Atlantic's beginnings is particularly romantic and remarkable. But if they were very young and a little naive when they began, Ahmet and Herb soon absorbed some of the necessary techniques of their competitors, even though they made surprisingly few records which neither of them liked. Personal taste wasn't generally considered a relevant factor by people working in the record business, most of whom disliked the music, despised the audience, and consequently treated the performers with little grace. They had too much else on their minds. Jerry Wexler, who didn't join Atlantic until 1953, had seen record people in action when he was working for publishers and for the music trade publication, *Billboard*.

"There was a kind of record man that was the *complete* record man, a Renaissance Man if you will, who did the whole thing. First, he had the brass to imagine that he could do it, that he could find somebody who would spend a dollar, a good, hard-earned American dollar, for his phonograph record. Then he had to find an artist, find a song, con the artist into coming into his studio, coax him into singing the song, pull the record out of him, press the record; then take that record and go to the disc jockeys and con them into putting it on the radio, then go to the distributors and beg them to take a box of twenty-five and try it out. That's the kind of experience that very few people get any more."

Most independent record firms started through a combination of accident, coincidence, and opportunism, often by people who owned record shops or a chain of juke boxes, who saw that the audience wanted certain kinds of music that existing companies didn't know about or disdained dealing with. Herman Lubinsky had a record shop in Newark, New Jersey, and in 1942 started the Savoy label and various subsidiaries to meet a demand for spirituals, blues, and bop jazz. A couple of years later, Ike and Bess Berman, who had a shop on 125th Street in Harlem, started the Apollo label with parallel lines to Lubinsky's.

With little formal education, and less concern for formal

contracts, most of the indie record men ran their financial affairs on a loose, day-to-day basis. If they had a credo, it was expressed by the owner who told a *Billboard* reporter, "The way an indie survives, you don't pay anybody." In particular, you didn't pay song writers or performers.

In the beginning, the owners' ignorance backfired on themselves: many of them didn't know that they could double their take by acting as publishers for the original songs written by their singers. Russ Sanjek, jazz collector and close friend of Jerry Wexler, held a job after the war at BMI (Broadcast Music Inc.), a rival publishers' collection agency to ASCAP (American Society of Composers, Authors, and Publishers). While ASCAP's catalogue consisted at that time mainly of "standards," BMI featured most of the hillbilly and blues songs, in addition to many recently composed pop songs. Sanjek saw that many of the independently-produced records mentioned no publisher on their label. "So I drafted a twenty-five-word telegram which I sent to the owner of any new record company that had a hit in the race market, inviting him to take out the publishing rights for his song, offering to send a contract."

Most owners took up the offer, but not all of them passed the good news about this extra source of income on to the people who wrote the songs. Often, in addition to claiming the two-cent publisher's royalty, the owner put his name on the record as co-writer, or even sole writer, and earned himself another cent or two on every copy sold. Occasionally, maybe to clear his conscience but more likely to make it all legal, the owner bought the rights to a song from the writer, paying ten or fifteen dollars for the copyright. Sometimes the writers didn't know they could expect far more in royalties if they kept the rights, but even if they did they often preferred to take fifteen dollars in bills while they were feeling thirsty, rather than wait six months for a few hundred—which would only come if their song was recorded and if it was a hit.

A probably apochryphal but nevertheless illustrative story about buying copyrights features Sidney Nathan, who operated King Records in Cincinnati from 1946 until he died in the mid-1960s. In the late 1940s, just before Hank Williams lit up the South, the number one country singer was Eddy Arnold, and number two was a King recording artist, Lloyd "Cowboy" Copas. Cowboy lived in Cincinnati, where he was a resident star on the local radio show "The Midwestern Hayride," but once a month he would go to Nashville to pick up some new songs. When he got back to Cincinnati, he would take them to Sid Nathan, who would pay half what Cowboy had paid, in return for which he got the publishing rights to them. So Cowboy was listed as composer, Lois Music as publisher, and everybody was happy, except maybe the writers, Pee Wee King and Redd Stewart, who got fifteen dollars a song for records which regularly sold 100,000 and on a couple of occasions over a million.

One month, Cowboy came back with a whole sheaf of really good songs, fifteen, maybe even twenty, all of them looking strong enough to record right away. Sid congratulated Cowboy on finding so many—all of them by Stewart and King—and almost as an afterthought asked, had Cowboy bought all the songs available?

And Cowboy said, "Well I got them all 'cept one, Mr. Nathan, but they wanted twenty-five dollars for it, which I didn't want to pay. Besides, I don't think it was as good as the others. It's called 'Tennessee Waltz,' and all it is, is a copy of Eddy Arnold's 'Missouri Waltz.' And I don't want people going round sayin' I'm followin' Eddy Arnold."

"Okay Copas, I understand," said Sid, "but I'm superstitious and I don't want to miss that one. So here's ten dollars and next time you go to Nashville, if they've still got it, buy it, and make up the difference with this."

Next month Cowboy came back from Nashville with some more songs from Pee Wee and Redd, and he laid ten dollars on top of them. Sid had forgotten about it. "What's that for?"

"That song you told me to buy, 'Tennessee Waltz.' "

"Oh, yeah." Sid picked up the money and put it back in his pocket. "They'd sold it, huh?"

"Well, no, Mr. Nathan, they hadn't. The bastards had put the price up to fifty dollars. And I wasn't going to pay that much."

Sid patted him on the back. "Copas, you done right. There ain't no song in the world worth fifty dollars."

The song became one of the best "copyrights" since the war (a "copyright" in music business jargon is a song that is recorded many times), and the story illustrates how mean and shortsighted Sidney Nathan was. But Sid himself would probably have defended his refusal to pay fifty dollars for just one song. "Tennessee Waltz" was a freak, and as Sid said, you can't go on freaks: "The record business is not a freak business. It's the same as the coffin business, or a funeral parlor."

When Nathan realized in the early 1960s that he might not recover from a bad illness, he make a twelve-inch LP record of himself giving advice to his employees at King—as a way of providing some guidelines on which to run the company after he was gone. In a brusque, rasping voice he laid down the principles of a successful firm: look for songs, not singers, and don't waste time with amateurs.

"When a song is brought to us, we have two answers. One answer has six words, and I quote: 'I think we can do something.' The other answer has two words, and I quote: 'can't use.' "

Nothing else need be said. "We are not here to soothe the feelings of starry-eyed amateur song writers."

One generalization could safely be made about all of the men who ran indie record firms: none of them were in business to soothe anybody's feelings.

THREE:
HOTEL OPERATORS

I

Ahmet was hard to interview. He was impatient with
the past, and preferred talking about tomorrow rather
than yesterday. He had just done interviews with a couple
of magazine writers. Besides, he was a very busy man.

Still, to everybody's surprise, he flew out to the Kal Rudman conference in Las Vegas. Rudman, now a professional
in the record business, is a qualified psychologist who used
to teach retarded and emotionally disturbed children—which he says was good training for dealing with
record people. Rudman worked as a folk music dee jay,
as a promotion man for Atlantic, and wrote columns in
which he tried to anticipate hits for *Billboard* and then
for *Record World* before he started his own "tip sheet,"
The Friday Morning Quarterback. Record companies and

radio stations subscribe to the *Quarterback,* generally rated third in terms of reliability and integrity (behind the tip sheets of Bob Hamilton and Bill Gavin), in order to keep track of which records are selling and/or being played in every locality across the States. Rudman spends every week on the phone to stores and radio stations researching his tips.

The idea of the Las Vegas conference was to produce a fruitful dialogue between record company promotion men and radio station program directors. But they never really got close to each other. Promotion men complained that some stations wouldn't even let them in the door, and program directors insisted that record companies were putting out too many bad records, and that they could only play records that the public was buying. Nobody seemed to expect to learn anything from anybody else. It soon became clear that most of them had come along for the evening entertainment, expenses paid.

The first night, there was a get-together of the Atlantic contingent in Jerry Wexler's room: various promotion men, plus Jerry Greenberg, the 29-year-old "boy" prodigy who heads the "second generation" Atlantic staff in New York, Earl McGrath, head of an incipient Atlantic subsidiary, Clean Records, and Marshall Chess, U.S. label manager for the Rolling Stones' label. Everybody sat around waiting for Ahmet.

He came in and the place came to life, but it wasn't clear why. He's not obviously hearty, or domineering, or lovable. He speaks in a slurred, rather whining voice that manages to make the listener aware of several backgrounds simultaneously: foreign, aristocratic, and streetcorner.

Almost immediately, the talk veered to reminiscences, and I offered to turn my cassette recorder off. Ahmet hadn't been aware it was on, and obviously didn't know who I was or that I was proposing to write a story on

Atlantic. But he said no, leave it on. For a while Jerry told
some of his apparently endless store of funny stories about
Ahmet's practical jokes, until Ahmet himself remembered
one that had involved Marshall's father, Leonard, whose
Chess company had been one of the major rivals to Atlantic
in the 1950s. Like most of the fables about Ahmet, this
one served to reveal how gullible and anxious most of
his competitors were.

"Leonard and Jerry and I were in Lindy's on Broadway,
along with Gene Goodman, who I couldn't stand because
he was in publishing. It was like two o'clock in the morning
and I'm drinking—you know, like, bring me a tray of
whiskey. And it was getting a little boring, nobody was
saying anything I hadn't heard before, so I said I've got
to make a very important phone call, and I went out and
came back and said I've got to go in a minute, to talk
to Ray Carroll.

"Now Ray Carroll had been a big jock in New York,
but now he had an all-night mood music show without
advertising—Percy Faith, albums. It was one of those things
where he'd put an album on and be on the phone to some
girl, and when the side finished he'd just flip it over and
go on talking to her.

"So I said to Leonard, who was from Chicago and didn't
know who was what in New York, I've got to go to see
Ray and I know I shouldn't have mentioned it, but I let
it slip that you were down here. And now it's gonna look
bad on you if you don't go up and say hello, you know,
when he knows you're in town. Leonard says, you goin'
up now? I say, yeah. He says, no, tell him I'll come up
tomorrow. I said, when he knows you could just take
the elevator up? Listen, that's Ray, of Willie and Ray—he's
got the hottest, most important radio show in New York.
So Leonard says, okay, expecting to hear some R and B.

"We go up and Ray's on the phone and this Mantovani

Crouching: Jerry Wexler (left) and Ahmet Ertegun (right) flank rock 'n' roll disc jockey Alan Freed at an awards ceremony. Joe Turner looks on from the back.

album is playing and we sit in a room where we can see Ray, and after about twenty minutes Leonard says, what's goin' on? I say, oh, you know, he's got a request . . . . they probably got somebody like Jimmy Martin here, paying him off. And he says, this Ray Carroll don't talk to you much, does he? So then Mantovani finishes and Ray, still on the phone, switches straight over to Percy Faith. Leonard says, hey, what's goin' on, he does no commercials. I say, he saves them up and does them altogether. After about two hours, Leonard finally realizes what's happened."

Every man who ever owned an indie company figures as the brunt of a story like that, in which Ahmet goes to amazingly devious lengths to waste their time and adrenalin. Yet hardly any of them seem to bear him any ill will, maybe because he achieved what all of them wanted, the presidency of a big record company, with control over secure stocks and a big salary to keep him in comfort for the rest of his life. But he must have gone a little too far with Morty Craft, somewhere along the line, because Morty really resents him.

II

Morty Craft is one of the first names to come up in conversations about New York record men who could be ruthless to do business with. Which is exactly how he likes to be known. "I had a house and yacht in Florida before Jerry Wexler knew where Florida was."

I met Morty Craft on the plane from Las Vegas to Los Angeles. I hadn't intended to go to Los Angeles, but all attempts to pin Ahmet down in Las Vegas had been foiled by distractions. Most of the time, I'd been content to trail around after him, getting a sense of who he was and how he worked. Learning little, slowly, Ahmet had a sure-fire system for winning at the roulette tables, which Marshall Chess and Earl McGrath were anxious to try out; they lost around $1,000 between them while I wondered who had the better attitude to money: they, who treated it as bits of paper to play games with, or I, who thought about the things I would have spent it on. Going back to my hotel the last night in Vegas, I noticed the first beautiful girl I had seen in two days there, a blonde with a wistful face. A man with huge sideburns sat next to her. When the same man sat next to me on the plane to L.A. the next day, I congratulated him on having found the best looking girl I'd seen in Las Vegas. "Yeah, nice kid, ain't she. College student. Got herself a fifty-thousand-dollar house from what she earns on weekends in Vegas." The man on the other side of me chimed in, "But the great thing about Morty is, after he'd finished with her, he sent her to me." I deduced that this was Morty Craft. "Yeah,"

Morty was glad to have his generosity appreciated. "Then I sent her down to a convention suite. She got a good haul, six guys at fifty dollars a throw."

All I knew about Morty Craft was that he had been owner of the Warwick label, which had Johnny and the Hurricanes, and before that the Melba label. But that was small fry. Morty was quick to fill me in on his more impressive activities:

"I was president of MGM in the Connie Francis era. We had Tommy Edwards, Conway Twitty. Then a different board was brought in, to run the movie side, and they kicked me out.

"I started out in the business as an arranger, at a time when there were just the major companies, and I worked mainly for Glenn Miller. Then I met a man called Dave Miller in Philadelphia, who picked up independently made masters and released them on his Essex label. He issued Bill Haley's first hit, 'Crazy Man Crazy.' Dave taught me the record business, the wheeling and dealing, and later I passed on what I knew to my assistant, Allen Klein, who made a fortune by applying what he had learned from working with me. I guess you've read about what he's done with Cameo, the Rolling Stones, the Beatles.

"After Essex, I started companies of my own, Melba—which had a hit by the Willows in 1956—and later Lance. I worked out an arrangement that became the song 'Alone,' which I recorded for the Shepherd Sisters. One of the Shepherd Sisters wound up marrying Jimmy Miller, the Rolling Stones' engineer and producer who lives in England now, I believe. But they got divorced.

"Art Talmadge at Mercury wanted to buy the master of 'Alone,' so I said if you do, you'll have to give me a job too, so Art hired me but he didn't have an office for me, so I was working from the hallway. I got the Diamonds to do the song 'The Stroll,' which was a million seller for them (with the help of Dick Clark), and then Arnold Maxin was leaving Epic to go to MGM and he took me with him. That was sometime early in 1958."

When the plane got to Los Angeles, Morty and I discovered that we were staying at the same hotel, the Continental Hyatt on Sunset. Ahmet and Jerry were on a different plane and staying at the Beverly Hills, where I had arranged to contact them later. As we drove off in a taxi, Morty said, "I could stay at the Beverly Hills, but who do I need to impress? Why should I spend a fortune, just to look good. There'll be a girl waiting for me at the Continental, young, charming, beautiful; she'll give me a rubdown, make me feel like a new man."

Why does he tell me all this? What is real? I don't ask; he goes on. "I have a party in the south of France, and flew some of the best looking girls in Sweden to it—blonde, over six foot tall. They don't do it for money, but because they like me. We have relationships, I get to know them, help them with their problems."

I ask for the rest of his career details. "I started Warwick in 1959 after MGM kicked me out, and apart from Johnny and the Hurricanes—whose records were all made by session musicians, by the way, the group just went on the road—I had the first hits from British-made records. Everybody said you couldn't sell British records in the States, but I did it with Petula Clark, Matt Monro, Andy Stewart. And I started Seven Arts around then too." Seven Arts is the company that bought up Warner Brothers before Warner sold out to Kinney. So Morty Craft had his fingers in that pie too? "Yeah, but that's another story."

He raced ahead to describe a year as head of Twentieth Century Fox's short-lived record label. "Mary Wells was coming up to her twenty-first birthday, so her contract with Motown would be up. Atlantic was after her, but I told her how if she signed with us she'd get movie contracts and be a real star. That wasn't in the contract, of course, but why should I feel sorry I tricked her; if she's so crazy with overblown ambition she deserves what she gets."

When we arrived at the hotel, sure enough, there was an attractive—not glamorous—girl in her early twenties, who obediently went with Morty up to his room to give him a rubdown. I went to phone the Beverly Hills to see if Ahmet was in yet.

III

Four days later, Ahmet took the cassette recorder's mike in his hand and began at the beginning. We were on a jumbo, flying back to New York from Los Angeles. He wouldn't have been on this particular flight at all if Mick Jagger hadn't decided to get married. Ahmet felt obligated to get to the wedding, partly because he fancied the idea of a society-type wedding in the south of France, partly because his pitch to the Rolling Stones to let Atlantic distribute their label had been along the lines of "Atlantic cares for its artists personally." Ahmet had to make it, even though it meant chartering a special plane from New York and missing at least one night's sleep because Ahmet's wife had a comparably important dinner party the day after, in New York. On top of which, Ahmet liked Mick.

Despite his best intentions, Ahmet hadn't been able to talk to me in Los Angeles. One of the innumerable distractions had been daily visits to Neil Young who was ill in hospital. Although Neil was signed to Reprise as a solo performer, he was tied to Atlantic as part of Crosby, Stills, Nash, and Young, having previously been a member of one of Ahmet's pet groups, the Buffalo Springfield. Hospital visits might help.

Sitting at the hospital bedsides of valued performers

was an Atlantic tradition that dated back to 1948, when Ahmet had to make hospital visits to one of the first artists he ever signed, Ruth Brown.

"Very soon after Herb and I decided to form Atlantic, the musicians' union declared a ban on all recordings, to start on January 1, 1948. So there we were with a record company and just a few months to go before a shutdown on recording. So we decided to stockpile as many records as we could, so that we would have something to sell in 'forty-eight. Most of the stuff we made was pretty bad, because we were having to record anybody we could find, without having much idea of how to shape it.

"It turned out that we needn't have worried. During the strike, people kept bringing us records which they said they'd recorded in South America, or two years ago. Before the ban. The musicians were out of work, and were doing little things by themselves.

"We recorded at Apex, and the first engineer we had was a little middle-aged German doctor, who didn't know anything about popular music but was technically reliable. For the second session, a kid walked into the studio. I said, 'Where's the engineer?' He said, 'I'm the engineer.' I kicked up a great fuss, saying, 'I will not have this child ruin my records.' But the owner insisted that this kid, Tommy Dowd, was fine—and of course since then Tom engineered almost everything we did."

A lot of responsibility rested with the engineer on independently-made records, where the aim was very often to reproduce the sound that a combo made on its live dates. The major companies, RCA, Decca, Columbia, were confecting pop music out of "nothing," bringing a singer to the studio, handing him a new song, and having the musicians play a formal arrangement for it. Because their attention was so taken up by the publishing houses that provided the material, and radio shows that introduced new singers, the majors more or less ignored the small-scale live entertainment in clubs and dance halls, which was what the indies began to record in increasing numbers from 1945 onward.

In the South, in Los Angeles, and in Chicago, much of this live music was blues-based, but in New York it was more sophisticated and jazz-oriented. So Atlantic, being based in New York, had a problem: both Herb and Ahmet liked jazz, and almost all the local musicians played jazz, but the black audience across the country preferred simpler blues.

"The first records we sold a few copies of were by Errol Garner, Joe Morris, Tiny Grimes, and Eddie Safranski. We tried to get them to do some kind of blues, but usually had to let them do three jazz numbers for every saleable blues. Joe Morris was the trumpet player out of the Lionel Hampton band, and he had Johnny Griffin on sax. We gave the title 'Lowe Grooving' to one of the numbers from his first session, which was named for a Washington disc jockey, Jackson Lowe. He played it quite a bit, and Waxie Maxie in Washington helped us a lot too, by playing our records on the radio show which was sponsored by his Quality Music Shop. In return we would give him free records. We sold between fifty and seventy thousand on four or five of the early records, and started getting listed in *Billboard's* 'Hot in Harlem,' which was a list of the local bestselling race records. 'Blue Harlem' by Tiny Grimes did well, with John Hardee on tenor sax.

"Everybody was discovering that it was a cheap business to get into, and local distributors would take a couple of hundred copies of each record because they knew they could get rid of that many of just about anything. And because we recorded some jazz, like Errol Garner, and we advertised the right way in the trades, we started to get a little prestige attached to our name, and also there was some publicity about my being Turkish. So we never really got desperate.

"I was living on fifty dollars a week, had moved out of Herb Abramson's closet and was living in a funky little hotel that was later condemned, the Jefferson, that was in the fashionable part of town, on Fifty-sixth Street. I paid about sixty dollars a week, half of which I paid, and the other half was paid by the company. We used the living room as an office, and I lived in the bedroom. And I was also still living in Washington, sharing an apartment with a Turkish diplomat, because I was still in graduate school.

"It was very useful to have the office in a hotel, because the hotel switchboard took messages, so it saved us from employing a secretary."

One of the records that helped to break Atlantic across the country was Stick McGhee's "Drinkin' Wine Spo De O Dee," a rollicking blues with an infectious chorus and an irresistible beat.

"One day I was on the phone to our New Orleans distributor. He was normally very cool and would rarely even accept my calls; when he did, it would be to order five of this, ten of that, we were a meaningless company to him. But this time he took my call, and while I was trying to get him to take a few of at least one of our latest releases, he said, 'There's a record out, on a label based either in Cincinnati or Harlem, called "Drinking Wine," by somebody called Stick McGhee. If you can find me five thousand copies of it, I'll really work on your record.' So I said send me a copy of it so I would know what to look for.

"He sent it up, and I listened to it, but I didn't know how to begin to look for five thousand copies of a cut-out record on a label I'd never heard of before, so I decided to do the record again, to copy it. The only guy I knew of in New York was Brownie McGhee, so I called him and said, 'Brownie, I'd like you to make a record for me; all you have to do is copy another record exactly.' He said, 'What's the song?' I said, 'It's called "Drinkin' Wine." ' He said, 'But that's my brother's record.'

"McGhee. For some reason it hadn't occured to me that there might be a connection. I said, 'Where's your brother?' He said, 'Right here.'

"So I had Stick come to the studio, and we spent about twelve hours trying to do an exact copy of the previous version. And I learned a lot about producing, just trying to reproduce exactly a sound that had been done before. And I don't know why, but we couldn't get it. Finally, we sent Stick home, and he came back the next day and did it almost straight away."

Herb Abramson, recalling the incident, had a slightly different story: "We got a message from a distributor in the South that there was a demand for a 'Drinkin' Wine Spo De O Dee' by Stick McGhee; I knew Brownie, and through him contacted his brother Stick, who had made the record for Mayo Williams' Harlem label, but had never got more than the ten dollar session fee. So Stick was happy to do it again for us, but although we spent all day trying to get the right sound, we couldn't get it, so I told them to sleep on it, come back tomorrow, and when they did, we finished it in about an hour."

The new version of "Wine-Spo-Dee-O-Dee" was easily the biggest seller yet for Atlantic, and it would have done better still if Ahmet and Herb hadn't neglected an important matter. Ahmet ruefully admitted, "We forgot about the original version. Next thing we know, Decca is competing with us. They had found Mayo Williams, bought up the rights to his version, and put it back on the market. But we outsold them, which gave us confidence in both our production techniques and our marketing."

They might not have spent so much time with that record, if Ruth Brown hadn't had a car crash. Ruth had been Atlantic's first big catch. Once established in New York, Ahmet had got a message from the Washington disc jockey, Willis Conover, to come down and hear Ruth sing with her husband Jimmy Brown's band at a club run by Cab Calloway's sister, Blanche, in D.C. Ahmet was knocked out by Ruth's singing.

"Dinah Washington was my favorite singer; she really killed me, and I'd been crazy about another singer who sounded like her—Little Miss Cornshucks. Well, Ruth Brown was in the same style, and I wanted to sign her. But Capitol had a guy down there too. So Blanche, who was Ruth's manager, had to choose between Capitol—already big with Nat Cole and all kinds of people—and a little label that had had about seven releases. But all our friends were there to persuade her to take a chance with us, and she did.

"So we booked Ruth into the Apollo, in the same week as Dizzy Gillespie, and we arranged to record her in New York. But on the way up, she and Blanche had an accident that laid Ruth in the hospital for nine months. And we paid the bills, although we could hardly afford it. But I was so grateful to her for signing with us, and she became a lifelong friend. Actually, by preference she would rather have recorded like Sarah Vaughan, but she didn't have the range for that, so we recorded her doing bluesier things.

"At the time that Ruth came out of hospital, and was getting ready to do our first session, Ernie Anderson, a guy who had been road manager to Louis Armstrong in the past, contacted us in connection with a movie short on the record business that he was producing for the *March of Time* series. He was going to do something on new companies in the program, and we could be the new company, but we had to record something by Eddie Condon. I said, 'Eddie Condon!' But I wanted us to be in the movie, so I said okay.

"A session in those days was four sides, so we did two with Condon, and two with his band backing up Ruth Brown. We did 'So Long,' and an original, 'It's Raining.' And the record sold quite well."

That was May 1949. If the company had folded after two years in the business, hardly anybody would have noticed.

FOUR:
THE SOUTH,
JESSE STONE,
AND THE BASS BEAT

I

The first decisive change in Atlantic's history came when Ahmet and Herb decided to go down South. Field trips through the major cities of the South were already an established procedure for several other independent companies, who would visit Houston, New Orleans, Memphis, etc., to promote current releases and look for new recording talent at the same time. On the West Coast, the owners of Aladdin, Specialty, Imperial, and Modern were making such trips regularly. Saul Bihari, one of three brothers who owned Modern (and its subsidiaries, RPM, Crown, and Flair), later recalled that the success of their business related directly to their activities in the South:

"We contacted Sam Phillips who had a little recording studio in Memphis, and Ike Turner, who was then a band leader who could always put together a session band. Through them, we recorded Howlin' Wolf, B. B. King, Rosco Gordon, Bobby Bland, Junior Parker, and a lot more. But we kind of lost contact. I guess we got a little lazy and didn't want to spend so much time on the road, and the next thing we knew all we had left was B.B. The others had signed up with Chess, Sun, or Duke.

"Years later, we were talking to Leonard Chess, and he told us that around 1950 he started realizing that here he was, five years in the record business and not getting anywhere. So he looked around to see who he thought was doing best in the area he was working in, and he chose us. So then he started asking around to find out what we were doing that enabled us to be so successful, and the answer was that we went around the South, meeting the jocks, finding new singers, keeping in close contact with the distributors. And that's what he started doing, right around the time we stopped. And he got to be more and more successful, while we weren't so consistent."

In New York, Ahmet and Herb listened to the records of these West Coast companies with envy and awe. John Lee Hooker, a guitar-playing blues singer who lived in Detroit but had an intense Mississippi style, was under contract to Modern; Lightnin' Hopkins, who had a cleaner-toned style of guitar playing, lived in Houston and recorded for Aladdin, a company that also featured the more sophisticated piano-playing blues singers Amos Milburn and Charles Brown. Specialty had the West Coast jump combos of Roy Milton and Jimmy Liggins, several great gospel groups, and contacts in New Orleans. Imperial had Fats Domino, whose first record, "The Fat Man," kept selling for months after its release in 1949. Atlantic's roster of performers couldn't command a large, reliable audience compared with all this. So in 1949 Ahmet commandeered a car.

"We were doing okay in New York, where we could keep on top of our distributors, and promote alongside them, keeping the disc jockeys friendly. Tiny Grimes and Joe Morris were selling as R and B, Garner as jazz. But we didn't have any singers. We were selling some records in New York, Washington, Chicago, and a few in Los Angeles and Cleveland, but we weren't selling any in the South, because we didn't have any blues singers—you just couldn't find blues singers in Harlem or Washington. They were all in Chicago, Texas, New Orleans. So, we realized we had to go down to the South, both to find new artists and record them, and to see our distributors down there.

"We weren't making any money—this must have been 1949—so we couldn't afford to take plane trips. But I had a friend, a very beautiful painter who was at Sarah Lawrence, who had been given a car by her parents and didn't know how to get it down to Texas where she lived. So I told her I would drive it down there. She thought this was very kind, and invited us to come and stay with her on her parent's ranch at Fort Worth. She didn't know we would do about eight thousand miles just getting down there, zig-zagging all over the place. She still doesn't know it, doesn't realize that without her car, we might never have got the company going."

One of the journey's missions, persuading distributors to take the Atlantic label, gave Herb and Ahmet the chance to introduce themselves, but Atlantic didn't carry anything they really wanted. Still, they made some finds.

"In New Orleans, we found Professor Longhair, and recorded him. He was playing at a club in a town where there were no white people at all. The cab driver wouldn't take us all the way there, but dropped us off on a road half a mile away, and we had to walk across a field to get to the place where Longhair was playing.

"It was packed like those pictures in cartoons, with people

hanging out all the windows. When we walked in, twenty people jumped out the windows because they thought we were cops. The only white people who ever went there were cops. We told them we were from *Life* magazine, because it wouldn't have meant anything to say we were from a record company."

II

The first trip South didn't have much immediate effect. A record by Blind Willie McTell, issued under the name of Barrelhouse Sammy, was released in January 1950, and a record by Professor Longhair was released the following month under the pianist's real name, Roy Byrd. But although they provided material to give the Atlantic label some credibility with southern distributors, they didn't have the impact of records by Fats Domino or Amos Milburn.

On the same trip, Ahmet and Herb bought some masters by several hillbilly singers, but although a special hillbilly series was started—the first release was a country version of "Drinkin' Wine Spo-Dee-O-Dee" by Loy Gordon and His Pleasant Valley Boys (Atlantic 721)—the line was soon abandoned.

Atlantic didn't pursue that first false trail into the country field, but they did try again with the southern blues. And on this next trip, Ahmet and Herb invited Jesse Stone to come with them: maybe he'd be able to figure out a way of taking advantage of southern music. He was, and music was never quite the same again. For Jesse Stone managed to find a way of writing down and reconstructing music that had previously been spontaneous and unpremeditated.

"Jesse Stone," says Ahmet, "did more to develop the basic rock 'n' roll sound than anybody else, although you hear a lot about Bill Haley and Elvis Presley.

"He was a great, reliable, loose arranger, who could update a five-year-old arrangement with a couple of chord changes. Those arrangements were very important, because although the record never came out exactly as the arrangement had been written, they gave something for everybody to hang onto."

"Jesse Stone," the alto sax virtuoso King Curtis recalled when I mentioned Jesse during a conversation in New York, "got me my first date on a New York recording session. Around 1954, not long after I'd come to New York from Texas, I was playing in a bar in midtown Manhattan, drums, piano, and me, seventy dollars a week. And this guy came in and said, 'What are you doing playing in a place like this?'

"I'd hear this all the time in those days. I think he'd been drinking quite a bit, and he didn't have any teeth because he'd just had them all pulled. So he was just a normal feller except he was a little more loaded, and he started telling me how he could do this and do that, and I was very polite, I always am in those situations, because you just never know who might turn out to be somebody.

"Anyway, sure enough the next night a guy comes in and says he's from RCA, and the day after that I was called in to do a session at RCA, signed a contract, and made eighty-two dollars and fifty cents for four and a half hours a week, where here I had been working seven and a half hours a night for seven nights for less than that, and having to pay the other guys in the band out of what I'd been getting. . . .

"Where's Jesse now? In New Jersey somewhere. I've never seen him with a girl past thirty. He plays piano with his latest discovery in little clubs near the race track in Jersey. You'll be able to contact him through Al Sears at Sylvia Music."

Sure enough, Al Sears (ex-sideman for Duke Ellington, later the leader of Alan Freed's band) had a phone number for Jesse, who agreed to meet me the next day outside the Sylvia office, 55th and Broadway. Looking much younger than he must be, fresh and fit, a copy of *Cash Box* and his brief case under his arm, he was right on time. We went to the nearest coffee shop.

I'd been a long distance fan of Jesse's from the first time I heard the Drifters' "Money Honey" and looked to see who wrote it; but I'd only discovered recently that Charles Calhoun, the writer of "Shake, Rattle, and Roll," was a pseudonym for Jesse. He pulled out a duplicated list of the songs he'd written under both names, dated back to the 1920s. Jesse linked them together:

"I was in the big band business for many years, had my own bands in Kansas, and later was with Ellington and Lunceford. Had a white girl band in Chicago for a while, the Coquettes. But then I came off the road, folded the band up in New York, and in the early forties I almost starved. That was when I wrote 'Idaho,' and 'Sorgham Switch,' which was a hit for Jimmy Dorsey, and quite a number of other songs that became hits. But at the time I didn't know where my next meal was coming from; I was having a *rough* time. Then RCA signed me up to do something like Louis Jordan was doing for Decca—novelty numbers with a jazz feeling. And I was signed to MGM. I almost had a hit, 'Smack Dab In The Middle.' I was recording then under the name of Charles Calhoun.

"I also did some freelance arranging, and I met Herb Abramson at National. Soon after he started Atlantic, he asked me to bring a vocal group I had been coaching, the Harlemaires, three boys and a girl, for a recording session, and that was a flop, but after that I would do occasional things for them."

In fact, Jesse wrote the tune for one of Atlantic's earliest national R and B hits, "Cole Slaw," a simple instrumental blues played by saxophonist Frank Culley.

"Then they went down South on a promotional trip, Herb and Ahmet, and they came back very excited about the sounds they'd heard down there and wanted to get on record. So the next time they took me with them to observe the music and maybe to figure out what we could try to do again in New York.

"We'd go down to New Orleans and put a sign outside that studio that was in back of a record shop, Cosmo's, yes, and we put a sign outside saying that on June twenty-second and twenty-third, or whatever the date was, the Atlantic Record Company would be there, and anybody with songs should bring them. We'd get a six-piece band in, and guys would line up outside like people going to a movie, with their songs, and they'd come in, and we'd audition them, have them tell us what key to play it in, work out an arrangement, and in half an hour we cut the song. We got a lot of material that way.

"When we got back from that first trip, I started writing. I had to learn rock 'n' roll—we didn't call it rock 'n' roll then—and it wasn't something that I could do easily at first. I considered it backward, musically, and I didn't like it, until I started to learn that the rhythm content was the important thing. Then I started to like it, and finally I started writing tunes. And I think I was one of the first people to write in a bass pattern, which was important for dancing—and I had always been a dancer.

"So when Atlantic signed up the Clovers and the Cardinals, I was assigned to rehearse them, get them ready for recording. A week or ten days before the session, I'd go down to Baltimore to work with them. The music I was trying to show them was based on the sound that I had picked up in the South, but they were northern boys and didn't feel it. They couldn't read music, which made it very difficult, and it took them six or eight months before we started getting hits. But then Atlantic signed Joe Turner, who I'd worked with before, and Ruth Brown started to be popular, and pretty soon we were getting at least one hit out of every session."

III

In fact, the first singer to benefit from Atlantic's experiments with the Southern Sound was Ruth Brown. Although she had six undistinguished releases first, Ahmet's hopes for her were finally realized in the success of "Teardrops From My Eyes," one of the biggest R and B hits in 1950.

"Teardrops From My Eyes" had a complicated arrangement, with horns weaving two separate riff patterns over a steady, even four-four beat from bass and drums. Ruth's voice was obviously controlled; she expressed her emotions through the tone of her voice rather than with sheer intensity, and despite the gloomy lyrics of "Teardrops" (by Rudolph Toombs), she didn't seem particularly upset. This character was reinforced on later releases, as Ruth dealt with all kinds of men and situations with a wry humor, a seductive catch in her voice, and a generally resilient tone that sometimes made her seem susceptible—to the right guy.

Meanwhile, Jesse Stone and the other arrangers used by Atlantic (unfortunately, no credits were given on the records) experimented with sounds to go behind Ruth.

"Shine On" had a clattering rhumba rhythm borrowed straight from Professor Longhair, and a sax break that sounded like something a New Orleans tenor man might have played. "5-10-15 Hours," recorded in 1952, had a smoother overall sound, but the rhythm was strong and steady; the following record, "Daddy Daddy" returned to a Latin-influenced rhythm, and then "Mama He Treats Your Daughter Mean" in 1953 had the drummer bash a tambourine close to the mike to make sure everybody noticed it was a dance song, while Ruth pushed her voice into more screeches than usual. The least sophisticated record of her career at that time, it was her biggest hit yet.

Ahmet and Herb had to draw what they wanted from Ruth Brown through an interpreter, an arranger who tried to submerge his preconceptions and apply theirs, using songs from outside sources (often Rudolph Toombs). But they worked more closely with the Clovers. At least Ahmet did, since he wrote some songs for them, and managed to get onto Atlantic the boogie sound that had intrigued him ever since the days in Washington when Albert Ammons, Meade Lux Lewis and Pete Johnson had played between sets by allstar jazz bands.

The left hand. A steady bass beat, a repetitive melodic figure. It surfaced on Atlantic records almost by accident, while the company was pursuing a different kind of music for a clearly growing market not yet supplied on the label: vocal groups.

Ahmet didn't like vocal groups to start out with; Herb didn't feel strongly one way or the other. They did scarcely anything in the field for the first three years, just an early record by the Harlemaires and a couple more by the Delta Rhythm Boys. Meanwhile the Jubilee label, which Herb had sold to Jerry Blaine, was becoming one of the hottest labels in New York because of the Orioles, a vocal group from Baltimore featuring the "so-cool" voice of Sonny Til.

It turned out that "Waxie Maxie" Silverman had a friend who ran a record store in Baltimore, Lou Krefitz, who

Faye Adams (inset, right) slipped through Atlantic's hands to enjoy three big R&B hits on Herald Records, while Ruth Brown (right) and the Clovers (above) became the foundation of Atlantic's early success. Smooth productions of well-crafted, often amusing songs gave them a dozen R&B hits each, which still sound good more than thirty years later.

tipped off Atlantic onto a good vocal group—the Clovers. Most groups of the period were made up of singers with little or no formal musical training, who often had limited vocal ranges, erratic pitches, and amateur notions of harmony. Ahmet didn't think much of them, but took a chance.

"The Clovers were against all the things I wanted to do. They liked the Ink Spots, who I didn't like at all, and they wanted to record 'Prisoner Of Love,' the Billy Eckstine song, but I was sure they wouldn't have a chance of selling many copies of it. So I wrote a song for them, 'Don't You Know I Love You.'

"No, it wasn't the first song I'd written. One of our early records was a thing I did for Billy Williams, an acrobatic saxophone player, called 'The Blues That Jack Built,' dedicated to a Washington disc jockey called Hal Jackson, who had a show called 'The House That Jack Built.' But that wasn't a proper song, it was just a riff really.

"But 'Don't You Know I Love You' gave me the courage to write other songs. The way the Clovers sang it was all wrong; I wrote it in a much blacker idiom than the way they sang it, which was more pop. There's a line in it, 'Baby, can't you see what you're doing to me?' I wanted them to go up at the end, high like a gospel singer; but they made it go down into a bass, so it had a novelty sound, more like the Ravens. But I must say they built the song into something, they contributed much more than I did.

"They didn't know they were coming to do a session; they thought they were coming to rehearse. The band I had booked didn't show up, but Frank Culley was playing at the same studio, and I asked him if I could use his rhythm section. He said, 'You use my rhythm section, you use me.' I said, 'But this is a vocal quartet record, Frank, they never have sax on them; you know the records, the Ink Spots, Orioles.' He was the kind of guy who never missed the chance to make a dollar, and he could see I was in a spot, so he said, 'Okay, I won't play—but you have to pay me, leader's scale, because this is my band.'

"So I said, 'Now listen, man, if I pay you, you're gonna play.' And he said, 'Okay, I don't mind playing.' We went down to the studio, and when the musicians set themselves up, there was no bass player. 'Where's the bass player?' 'Oh, he didn't show up.'

"So we had to do the session with no bass player, but with a sax. So that's how a vocal group record got a sax on it. I forget what we did about the bass, the guitar player just used his bass strings or something."

From the sound, there was no guitarist there either, just brushed drums, Frank Culley honking sympathetically and atmospherically all the way through, and a pianist whose left hand was just like Jimmy Yancey's. This strong instrumental background, and the unusual bluesy tone of the lead singer's voice, set the record apart from contemporary vocal group records by the Orioles and the Five Keys, whose accompaniment and overall sound were lighter, more ethereal.

"Don't You Know I Love You" was one of the biggest R and B hits of 1951, and was followed by a long string of successive hits for the group. Ahmet wrote a couple more, and Rudy Toombs contributed some songs with stronger lyrics that did just as well—"One Mint Julep," and "Crawlin'."

While Ahmet's pianist was recording Yancey-like boogie on the Clovers' records, Yancey himself was ill in Chicago. Ahmet made arrangements to go there and record him. "I went to Maxwell Street, and as I walked down it, all the stallowners who sold records were playing the Clovers on their little portable record players. It was one of the great moments of my life to see all those people dancing to a record I had made. To think that so many black people would dance to my record."

Jimmy Yancey was well enough to do a session with

Ahmet, but he brought along some reinforcements just in case. He came with two or three other piano players, Little Brother Montgomery and a couple of others. "I asked him why they'd come, and he said he'd told them to come in case he wasn't well enough to play, so that we'd be able to record somebody and wouldn't have wasted our time. He played some beautiful things that day—have you heard the LP we put out with that session on it? Jimmy plays one side and his wife Mama sings on the other."

Meanwhile, Atlantic also recorded the Cardinals in a style that was closer to the accepted vocal group pattern: wavering lead singer backed by more or less spontaneous sounds from the backup singers. This urban folk music depended heavily on the ability of the singers to convey a natural presence. If the harmonies were too slick, or the musical arrangements too clearly arranged, the illusion of intimacy and sincerity was lost. "Shouldn't I Know" by the Cardinals met most of the standards of the genre—although the guitarist was a lot more imaginative than usual for this kind of record—and it was a hit; so were several more by the group, but Atlantic didn't feel proud of them, and now Ahmet can't remember the names of any of the singers. Even for Jesse Stone, they were just a group he coached, nothing special.

But Joe Turner they remembered well, and proudly. Ahmet had signed him at an opportune moment. "James Rushing had left Count Basie, and so they hired Joe Turner, and I went to the first show they did together, at the Apollo. And Count had those tricked-up arrangements. They'd been doing numbers like 'Don't The Moon Look Lonesome Shinin' Through The Trees,' for fifteen years, so they could play about with the arrangements, extend the middle section by ten bars, stuff like that. Which Jimmy Rushing had been living through, right?

"So Joe Turner came in, and he wasn't that kind of singer. He was the greatest blues singer, Kansas City style

*Joe Turner. A "fanzine" editor asked him how he
wrote "Boogie Woogie Country Girl," and was told:
"I walked down the street and sang it to myself;
I take it home to the hotel, lay down and listen
to it, put the TV on awhile, run down the street,
a few hot dogs, come back and listen awhile, go
in a bar and drink a li'l wine, come back, go
down the street again, look around, go downtown
to a picture show, bump around all over New York,
all the time singing the song, I call Atlantic and
tell 'em I'll be ready in a coupla days. We go
on down the studio, make the arrangements, make
the music, set it up and it is just perfect." (From
an interview in* Rollin' Rock.)

blues singer of them all. He has a voice that nobody can match.

"But, Joe and Basie never got together. The band would finish and Joe would still be singing, you know. I'd heard that Columbia had dropped Joe, and although his arrangement with Basie was that he would only record with the Basie band, that sort of fell apart. I took him to a bar after the show, and he was feeling very depressed, but we knew each other from the old days, and finally I said, 'Listen, come with us, and we'll make hit records.' And he said, 'All right, Cous, I'll go with you and see what happens.' He always called me 'Cous.'

"So I wrote 'Chains Of Love' with Van Walls; well, actually, I wrote it, but I gave half to Van Walls because he played the piano introduction." ("Chains Of Love" was originally going to be called "Three O'Clock Blues"; according to Jerry Wexler it was a rewrite of "Mecca Flat Blues.")

Not many companies at the time would have given half the composer royalties to an outstanding session musician, but Van Walls certainly deserved it for his piano playing. Van Walls, whom Ahmet remembers as an eccentric who dressed like Sherlock Holmes—a black Sherlock Holmes— came to Atlantic out of Frank Culley's band. His complicated but fluid and sympathetic accompaniments distinguished Atlantic's blues ballads from everyone else's, and were unmistakable features of Joe Turner's first three hits, "Chains Of Love," "Sweet Sixteen" (also written by Ahmet), and "Still In Love" (by Doc Pomus). All three were slow blues, characterized by Joe's extraordinary resonant voice, which implied gentle rocking rhythms without obvious emphasis.

IV

By 1953, Ahmet and Herb had assembled a team of the best session men in New York. If Jesse Stone wasn't available, they could call on Howard Biggs or Budd

Jesse Stone. The writer of "Money Honey" and "Shake Rattle and Roll," whose arrangements enabled New York session men to get to grips with rock 'n' roll.

Johnson to arrange the music. Sam "the Man" Taylor played a hard-driving saxophone; he was recruited when Herb and Ahmet went looking for somebody who could play tenor sax like Maxwell Davis on Amos Milburn's records on Aladdin. When they wanted a tenor sax with a softer tone, to go with Ruth Brown's voice, for instance, Budd Johnson would play the breathy solos, until Ruth brought her boyfriend along to one session and insisted he accompany her. That—according to Jerry Wexler—is how Atlantic got introduced to Willis Jackson, who was used regularly after that.

Mickey Baker was Atlantic's guitarist, whose decisive phrases and slightly brittle tone have hardly dated at all; before they started using him, their records all had a guitar sound that reeked of the 1940s and "jazz." Mickey played the blues. Connie Kay on drums and Lloyd Trotman on bass completed the ideal rhythm section, with Henry Van Walls playing piano on numbers where there was room for idiosyncratic accompaniment, and Ernie Hayes coming in where an arrangement needed to be followed more precisely.

Hardly any of these crucial men were under contract. Robert Townsend, author of the guide to progressive management, *Up The Organization,* would have been impressed: "Without employment contracts, the company must keep the climate challenging and invigorating and the rewards commensurate with the performance. Contracts in my opinion usually lose the men they are designed to hold. And keep those who have no other basis for staying."

Musicians and song writers liked to work with Herb and Ahmet, who respected them, gave them challenges, and paid them. The only people under contract were a few of the performers, Tiny Grimes, the Joe Morris band, Joe Turner, Ruth Brown, the Clovers. Van Walls was too, but as a featured performer on his own records. They seem to have honored their contracts, a sign that they felt some commitment to Atlantic. On the West Coast, where most of the performers were convinced that record companies weren't paying them all the royalties they were due, singers often recorded for anybody who would put up a little money in front, regardless of whatever "exclusive" contract they might have signed. And according to Ahmet, it wasn't only the indies who were robbing artists:

"I'll never forget, after we'd been going a year or two, a senior staff man came to me from Columbia Records. He said, 'Listen, we've been watching you, and we think you're making some pretty good product. And we'd like to take you over.' I said, 'Really? On what basis?' He said, 'How about if we give you a two percent royalty, out of which you can take care of the artists.'

"I said, 'Take care of the artists? We're giving *them* three to five percent.' And he said, 'So it's you that's been spoiling it for everybody.' "

The big companies—Decca, Columbia, RCA—hadn't been paying the black artists any royalties on sales. Black song writers were lucky if they ever got composer credits or song writing money; the publishers would usually cop that. Consequently, the big companies often had trouble finding the artists when they wanted them for a recording session.

"By offering the black artists the same kind of terms that RCA would be offering to their top white artists, we were able to draw good performers." This was Ahmet's recollection of Atlantic's early policy on contracts and royalties, but a music business lawyer who represented performers in those years was skeptical. "I wouldn't take my artists to Atlantic then. They might have honored their royalty agreements, but the rates were so low, it hardly made any difference. Other companies paid more in advance, which was what we were looking for."

One sore point in the Atlantic story, for Herb Abramson

anyway, was the way Atlantic let the Joe Morris band out of its contract and so lost a big hit, "Shake A Hand." In 1953 Herb received notice that he was to spend two years' service as a dentist to the American Armed Forces in Germany, fulfilling the terms of the government training plan that had funded his years at dental school. One of the last things he worked on before he left was a song that the Joe Morris Orchestra was planning to record with one of the band's vocalists, Faye Adams. Herb supervised rehearsals of the song in Montgomery, Alabama, while waiting to be sent overseas, but he couldn't stay long enough to make sure it was recorded. Joe Morris grew impatient waiting for someone else at Atlantic to make the record and asked Al Silver at Herald Records to do it, thereby giving Al the biggest R & B hit of 1953.

FIVE:
TIME TO WORK,
TIME TO PLAY

I

Jerry Wexler prowls around his bedroom, pulling socks and shirts out of drawers, packing a case for the drive up North. "Did you see that magazine article where some kid called Leonard Chess a tyrant and an exploiter? Man, I get sore as hell when these young writers come sailing in with stuff like that. Leonard's dead! That writer never met him. How does he know what kind of guy Leonard was? Have you heard those Chess Records? Hey man, that's a treasury of folk music there, all those Muddy Waters, Howlin' Wolf records. Did you hear that album they just put out by Jimmy Rogers, who used to be a sideman in Muddy's band? It cooks better than Sonny Boy."

I've only just met him, but already a man of wide interests and fierce emotions is declaring himself. Jerry seems to read every music paper in the country, and gets upset every time writers with little knowledge of rock's background reveal their ignorance, or prejudice. Unlike many record company executives, he listens to music for pleasure. And, where I had expected him to be critical of the dubious business practices of rival record companies, he comes to the defense of men he regards as fellow professionals. Isn't it true that Leonard Chess didn't pay his artists everything he owed them?

"Maybe. But he recorded them, that's what's important. Sure, he treated them differently from the way we treated our artists. There was a story that another record company owner went to visit Leonard at his home, and was shown into a room where he was asked to wait for Leonard. So he sat down, and read a magazine. A black guy was painting the window frames, and he started singing, till the record man said, 'Hey, you're pretty good. You could make a record.' The guy said, 'I already have,' and the record man said, 'Oh yeah, what's your name?' And the guy said, 'Muddy Waters.' "

Jerry wasn't sure if his feelings about Leonard Chess should be quoted. "It wasn't my place to say anything to Leonard about the way he treated his artists; Leonard told me he had an agreement with Muddy, that if Muddy's records stopped selling, he could always come work for Leonard at his house. I said, 'Oh yeah? That's funny, because Joe Turner and I have the same kind of deal. Joe told me, if our company ever gets into trouble, I can always get a job as his chauffeur.' "

The suitcase packed, we proceed to Jerry's office: one end of a long room that runs from a pool table at the front door, past a big settee and mirror wall, to sliding glass panels that look out onto the swimming pool and beyond to Jerry's boat. This is one of three permanent Wexler residences, the winter home. "It's the plum I award myself for working hard all my life. And I have worked hard, and I'll go on working hard. But I wanna do it from now on in circumstances that groove me, where it's warm and there's sand and palm trees while there's snow storms in New York, where it's slowly turning into a stinking compost heap. So I set it up here, with an arrangement at Criteria Studios where we have first option on one of the two studios, and where the artists love to come, by the way, especially in wintertime. It's an indulgence."

But there is a strong element of function in Jerry's sense of comfort. The Florida house has a direct line to the New York office, and there are extension phones everywhere, even by the swimming pool where Jerry can take calls by plugging a phone jack into a wired-up tree. The move to Miami did not mean isolation from the record business. Among the local residents is Henry Stone, a veteran indie operator who currently distributes several major companies through Florida, and also has his own labels. The biggest recent hit for Stone was Betty Wright's "Clean Up Woman" on his Alston label, distributed nationally by Atlantic. There's a Betty Wright record on Jerry's desk.

I look at the label. "J. P. Robinson's on Alston, too. Have you heard him?" Jerry says yes, why? "He's good, sounds like the kind of person Elton John wishes he were. John Abbey likes him a lot too, has raved about him a couple of times in *Blues and Soul*." *Blues and Soul* is a British biweekly magazine devoted to current R and B releases, and provides information for the small but devoted fans of soul music in Britain. Since the American rock press more or less ignores R and B releases, Jerry values the attention paid to the music closest to his heart, even in so distant and obscure a publication. "Do you think I should sign him up?"

I assume the question is academic, but say yes. Jerry reaches for the phone and dials a number. "Henry? This is Jerry. What's J. P. Robinson doing? I'm gonna sign him to Atco, we'll pay you eight thousand, and eight percent, okay? Yeah, we'll put him with Brad and Dave."

I'm taken aback; how can a company function with such off-the-cuff decisions? What kind of budget is allocated to signing up new acts?

"Budget, man we never had a budget. Never had a recording production budget, a promo budget, a publicity budget. The Kinney company had a fit when they saw how we operated, but they accepted it."

It had always been like that. "In the old days we used to have to go to the bank to see if we had enough money to make a session. That all changed in fifty-eight—Bobby Darin and Leiber and Stoller. Until by sixty-four, when we were getting impatient that we were making all this money for the company and we weren't getting much for ourselves. So we decided to sell the publishing company, Progressive Music, so we could buy ourselves some home comforts."

Eventually they sold Atlantic itself to Warner Brothers; within a few months Warner had been taken over by the Kinney Corporation, a rent-a-car and parking lot conglomerate. "We valued the security those deals offered us. A lot of money, annual salaries. Did we give up our autonomy? Yes, because once we sold, we could never claim total autonomy, because somebody else holds the shares. We maintain our autonomy because we perform, we do what we were expected to do, run a successful record company. As long as we make the right decisions, nobody is going to question the way we arrive at them." No pressures from Kinney?

"Of course I have read the same things you've seen, but in all our dealing with them we have found them to be very nice people, very honorable, very fair."

Now part of the Kinney family, Jerry does brotherly

favors for people on the other Kinney labels. Reprise's Little Richard, who is recording at the Criteria Studio in Miami, plans to bring a tape of the session to Jerry's house this evening to hear Jerry's comments.

But meanwhile, it's teatime. Shirley Wexler prods her husband into telling stories. Jerry and Shirley have three children, all away at school or college. Not long ago Jerry visited his daughter Anita's college on the West Coast to address a seminar group on the subject of producing records. He had hardly begun when he was interrupted by a student wanting to know "how come you're ripping off our culture?"

Addressed to almost any other record company vice-president, the question would have been a tricky one. But the kid hadn't done his homework. Jerry looked at him. "What do you mean, your culture? It's *my* culture." Jerry's conversation, laced as it is with the jargon of recording studios, radio announcers, and ghetto streets, is evidence enough.

"One time Ahmet and I were in L.A., visiting our distributor, Jim Warren, at Central Records. They have all the R and B lines, Specialty, Imperial, Apollo. So Ahmet calls Imperial and gets Lew Chudd on the phone. All the salesmen are standing around, on the extension phones, listening. Lew Chudd has no sense of humor at all, very stiff.

"Ahmet gets him on the line. 'I wanna speak to Chudds. Lemme speak to Chudds.'

"Lew holds the phone. 'This is Mr. Chudd.'

"'Yeah, Chudds. I'm Alvin Domino, Antoine's uncle. [Fats Domino's real name was Antoine.] I'm in town and I thought I'd come over to see you.'

"'I see. Well it's getting late, and I'm pretty busy. What's on your mind? Can I help you in some way?'

"'Yeah, you can help me. You got an expensive town here. I think I'll come over and get a little taste.'

" 'What do you mean, a taste? You want an advance, out of Fats' royalties?' But Lew's voice gives away that he's stalling.

" 'Oh, never mind, man. That's cool, whether you wanna charge it to Antoine or pay it out of your own pocket. 'Cause I want you to know that I used to dangle Antoine on my knee when he was a little boy, and he's tired of his gig over here.'

" 'What do you mean?'

" 'Well he don't like the way you're payin' him.'

" 'I beg your pardon, we pay our performers fair. You can check with BMI.'

" 'Oh, don't give me none of that BM an' I, IB an' M—you jivin' that boy. And when his contract's up, I'm gonna see to it that he gets with a good label.'

" 'What are you talking about, who you gonna put him with?'

" 'I'm gonna put him with Atlantic.'

" 'Atlantic! They wouldn't do that.'

"'What do you mean, they wouldn't. That bald-headed Turkish cat, and that Jew! I thought you were foolish before, and now I *know* you're stupid.'"

II

Little Richard comes around with three other men. One of the men is his old producer from the Specialty days, Bumps Blackwell; the others are musicians who have been backing Richard on the session. One of the scheduled musicians showed up two hours late, so they've done much less than planned. Jerry threads the tape of the session onto his machine, and we listen.

It's "Shake A Hand," the same song that Atlantic "lost" years before when Joe Morris was allowed to take Faye

Adams and the song around the corner to Herald Records after rehearsing the arrangement under Herb Abramson's supervision in Montgomery, Alabama. This version is sung well by Richard with sympathy for the words and good control of his voice. The accompaniment is spare, just a basic rhythm track and good guitar. "I'll sweeten that a little," Jerry promises as it finishes.

Sweeten it. The expression exactly fits the process it describes. After the voice and rhythm track have been "laid down" onto tape, the package is handed to an expert arranger who fits in the extras: horns, strings, voices, or all three, depending on the kind of record, the budget available, the nature of the vocal performance. I argued with Jerry that he uses too much sweetening too often on Atlantic records, as if he doesn't think the lyrics and the singer are good enough to stand unadorned. To me, the process is the same as women applying makeup: I go for natural beauty, and if makeup is used, it shouldn't be obvious. Little Richard doesn't mind the sweetening, and seems happy as he hands over the tape to let Jerry do with it whatever he chooses. But then, he wears makeup too.

From the reports of his stage act, TV appearances, and interviews, I'd expected Richard to be a high-camp fag, but although he is wearing a loose-fitting green outfit that shows plenty of skin, he talks seriously and unself-consciously about his recording session. I corner Bumps Blackwell to ask about the classic records he made with Richard in the mid-fifties. Bumps recalls hearing Ray Charles' "I Got A Woman."

"I couldn't get over it. He'd taken a gospel song that Alex Bradford had recorded for Specialty and made it into an R and B number. But we couldn't do that kind of thing at Specialty, because Art Rupe was always worried about the reaction from the religious people—he had a big line in gospel records. I guess Atlantic could do it because they didn't have any gospel sales to lose.

"Art never would let us make that crossover from gospel to pop. I wanted to record Sam Cooke doing pop, I was sure he could be as big as the Platters, and I arranged a session for Sam to cut a song called "You Send Me." Art came into the studio in the middle of the session, saw the white girl backup vocal group I had in there, and he wanted to break it up.

"I was sure that Sam would be big, and insisted that I finish the session, but Art didn't want any part of it, so finally he said he would never put the song out on Specialty, and I said that I would buy Sam's contract from him and take the song somewhere else. So we reached an agreement where I forfeited the royalties Art owed me from previous records, in return for Sam's contract and mine. And I took 'You Send Me' down the street to Bob Keene, who put it out and made the top of the chart."

"Yeah," growled Jerry. "You didn't ask us if we wanted it. Sam Cooke was our kind of singer; all you had to do was pick up a phone."

Too late for Sam Cooke now. But there's still room for a deal. Atlantic has recently started a gospel series—possibly to placate black spokesmen who accuse Atlantic of "ripping off" the black culture without contributing anything valid to it, but also as a way of discovering good new singers before they cross over out of gospel: every good soul singer once sang in church. Bumps is representing a number of major West Coast gospel acts. He and Jerry make a verbal agreement to put some of Bumps' acts in the Atlantic series.

Business over, Richard, Bumps, and the musicians leave, and Jerry gets on the phone to the musician who held up the recording session. "Jesse? This is Jerry. Man, what's goin' down? Richard was here, and he told me that you were two hours late for the session. Man, you can't do that, you're spending Richard's money, and keeping the other guys hangin' around with nothin' to do.

"Man, there's time to work, and time to play. Hey, I know, man, we all got problems, but we also got a job to do, and we have to do one thing before the other. I know this has got nothing to do with me, but you can't just leave your wife and kid with nobody lookin' after them."

Jerry cannot avoid sounding the white boss to the black employee, no matter how hard he tries to make it man-to-man and hip jive. But he knows that, and here it isn't a thick-skinned boss man talking, but somebody with a team of musicians he's proud of and wants to hold together. And the team of musicians who work on Atlantic sessions at the Criteria Studios isn't just a bunch of the best hand-picked men in the South, but people Jerry cares about for one reason or another. Mac Rebennack, for one.

Mac Rebennack wouldn't be in Florida, working at the studios, if Jerry hadn't gone to some trouble to extricate him from California, where he was sinking in debts mysteriously accumulated by people living at his expense. Now Mac, who records under the name Dr. John the Night Tripper, is installed in Miami. Tonight, he's coming around.

III

Mac Rebennack is extraordinary. He cracks up into a fit of delighted giggles at the slightest joke, is the most benign guy I ever met and yet reveals a considerable background of musical history as he talks in an idiosyncratic Cajun accent. Jerry sits him at the piano and suggests I turn my cassette recorder on, and for the next couple of hours Mac gives an illustrated dissertation on New Orleans music. Mac's story takes in disc jockeys and distributors, record company bosses and jazz clarinettists, but focuses, naturally enough, on piano players.

By far the most famous New Orleans piano player is Fats Domino, who had an almost unbroken series of R and B and rock 'n' roll hits through the 1950s. His name comes up a few times, but chiefly as a popularizer; as an innovator or a technician, he doesn't even get on Mac's list. "Remember Fats' first record, 'Fat Man'? He was trying to play 'Junkie Blues' the way 'Fess did it, which wasn't as good as the way Champion Jack did it."

But if Champion Jack Dupree was the man who was most responsible for creating the typical New Orleans piano sound of left-hand chords following a boogie type of rhythm, he didn't stick around in the city to develop it, and the two piano players Mac remembers best were 'Fess (Professor Longhair) and Archibald.

Jerry remembers Longhair too: "He used to keep time by kicking the piano, and he put his foot right through the side on a session he did for us."

Mac laughs. "Yeah, I never seen a piano as broke and out of tune as the one he played on Joe Ruffino's records. He used to play a funny way, man, with one of his fingers crossing over like this. I don't know how he could do that. Him, Jessie Hill, and Mel Lastie, they all had the joint on this finger shaped like a triangle, and bigger than all the other joints. I always figured they must have been from the same tribe."

Mac plays the classic Longhair tune, "Goin' to the Mardi Gras," with all the flourishes that characterize the record, and the same compulsive rhumba rhythm. Then he comes back to Joe Ruffino, who owned the Ric and Ron labels in the late fifties whose distribution was limited to New Orleans on most records.

"I had wrote some helluva tunes for Joe when I was his assistant A and R man or something, for Johnny Adams. But Joe had it figured out some kind of a way so he made money off all his records but nobody else did. Like I had this song for Johnny, 'Losing Battle,' boy that was a hot record, I knew I had some money coming off that one—not a cent. The next one came out, 'Showdown,' and boy, that was even hotter than 'Losing Battle.' I *knew* I had somethin' comin' in on that one. Not a cent."

I asked if anybody did pay royalties in those days. "Yeah, there was two. Venice Music, and Atlantic. (Venice was Specialty's publishing firm.) I would get checks, man, through the mail. You never heard of that. You figured you were lucky if you got paid for playing on sessions. Johnny Vincent would have a session for somethin' he was doin' on Ace, and you'd go along and hope you got paid for the date."

Mac is mystified that I like so many of the records made in New Orleans at that time. So far as he can remember the musicians were so high on most of them that they didn't know what key the song was in. But one I had always liked, which definitely sounded as if the musicians knew what they were doing, was Jerry Byrne's "Lights Out," for Specialty, on which Mac was co-writer. I asked Mac whatever happened to Jerry Byrne.

It seems Mac had organized a band that could change its colors on request. Jerry Byrne "used to sing with my band. We used to play around New Orleans and along the Coast, and the posters would advertise two or three different bands. There'd be Frankie Ford and the Thunderbirds; and Jerry Byrne and the Loafers—we got that name because Jerry worked in a shoe store on Saturdays selling loafers. And some other names like that. But really, it was just my band with different singers." Sometimes they even passed themselves off as famous singers, and "we'd be advertized as Bobby Rydell, and Frankie Avalon, and Chuck Berry. Earl King, he'd do Chuck Berry, and he was real good, doin' the duck walk an' all of that. But Jerry got into some trouble and had to go off-the-set for a while. That was a real shame, man, because his record was just starting to sell, and they took it off the air."

The name of Ray Charles comes up for the second time that evening. Ray's role as a musical innovator was not widely appreciated until the early sixties, when his "soulful" voice sold millions of records and inspired a number of younger singers to adopt an extravagant, passionate style; notably Eric Burdon and Joe Cocker. But Ray Charles made his decisive contribution to music while recording for Atlantic in 1953 and 1954. Previously he was a soft-voiced singer and light-fingered piano player in the popular "West Coast school." But during 1953 he played in New Orleans and the South, where he picked up much of his gospel-based singing and chordal piano playing from the local stars there. To illustrate the change, Mac plays the freer West Coast style of Lloyd Glenn and Charles Brown to show what Ray had been doing in the late forties, and then shifts to the more rhythmic, percussive style of New Orleans pianist Huey Smith, to show the change that Ray had had to make. Bringing a highly developed technique to the New Orleans style, Ray was able to sound original, and make musical innovations. But there was no doubt about his sources; Mac plays a Guitar Slim song, "Feelin' Sad," with piano accompaniment as Huey Smith had played it; and then the same song, as played and sung by Ray Charles. "Ray brought the piano part that Huey had in the chorus, put it at the start, and played it this way; Huey could never have got around those chords like that." Mac chuckles, and by the end of the evening I understand why Jerry has such affection for him. I wish that Mac's records as Dr. John the Night Tripper would com-

Mac Rebennack, with beads in his hat, voodoo charms around his neck, and gris gris in his beard: Dr. John the Night Tripper. An outstanding contemporary session keyboards player, he served his apprenticeship as a member of the Funk Club, a clique of New Orleans musicians who played on almost every record made in New Orleans during the late fifties, and the music he plays today represents much of what Jerry Wexler prefers to listen to.

municate more of the person he is, and be less concerned with the mysteries of creole voodoo.

A year later, in April 1972, Atlantic issued an LP of Mac as Dr. John playing his versions of standard New Orleans R and B songs, staying close to the originals by Professor Longhair, Archibald, James Wayne and others. Called *Gumbo,* the LP was a remarkably accurate evocation of the city's best musical spirit.

After a couple of hours of Mac's talking and playing, Jerry and I go play billiards. While Jerry shows some good shots that expose my own clumsy fumbles, Mac plays on, classic New Orleans piano. For a moment there, I'm in High Society.

IV

During the next couple days of my stay with Jerry and Shirley, the parade of visitors and flow of telephone calls never slows down. The pace is impressive but also a sign that Jerry hasn't managed to delegate responsibilities properly. Though only in his early 50s, he has the bearing of an older man: the archetypal Jewish patriarch. As if to foster this image, he has grown a beard, mostly silver gray. Padding around the house in shorts, he is simultaneously Ernest Hemingway and the Old Man in Hemingway's story of the sea. Actually, Jerry himself had a fight with a fish recently. An eight-millimeter home movie shows the moment a few weeks earlier when Jerry struggled in vain with a huge fish that took the bait on a rod too small to carry its weight. Jerry, while sitting in a small collapsible chair, held it for more than an hour before the line snapped and has needed treatment on his back ever since. Maybe that contributes to his worn-out appearance.

Yet it isn't easy to see what he could pass onto other

shoulders, so long as he wants to be part of the Atlantic administration. For part of Atlantic's character results from the refusal of the senior staff to accept the conventional pyramidal structure of decision making normal in firms with a turnover as big as Atlantic's. When Jerry signs a performer up, he doesn't just pass the singer onto a producer and wait until the record is pressed; he asks for tapes of everything the producer does, as he records it, the basic tracks, the final mix with sweetening, the rejected songs that the producer didn't consider worth issuing. Jerry sends back his comments, dubs copies onto cassettes on his own sound system, and sends them off to people in the New York office. If it's something he is particularly enthusiastic about, he gets acetates made and mails them off to his favorite disc jockeys across the country, giving them exclusive records in their own cities, and generating advance interest in the record.

All this may be admirable for a man who could be sitting comfortably in the sunshine with a large salary more or less guaranteed, but, depending on where you sit, it can also be an irritating distraction that unsettles everybody—from the producer who feels that he isn't being completely trusted to deliver a good tape, to the pressing plants, to the New York office who don't feel fully in control of the promotion they've been nominally delegated to handle, to the disc jockeys who didn't get advance acetates and who might hold back from playing the record when it does get officially released and mailed to them.

So, among those who still work for Jerry Wexler, or have worked for him in the past, there is a curious mixed response—of admiration, affection, and respect on the one hand, and resentment that can come close to hatred, on the other.

SIX:
THAT'S FUN, RIGHT,
SELLING RECORDS?

I

Jerry came out of the same sort of musical background as Ahmet and Herb, a passionate jazz fan who could identify backup musicians on records. But whereas Ahmet and Herb had at least satisfied their parents by going through college in a more or less orderly fashion, Jerry was every mother's nightmare son. He graduated from high school early, at 15, and then bounced from City College to N.Y.U. to Kansas State before dropping out altogether in 1937. Classrooms gave him claustrophobia. From then until he was drafted in 1944, he has a difficult time accounting for himself. He can remember hanging out, doing odd jobs, listening to jazz.

"During the day," Jerry recalls, "we'd go to the Museum of Modern Art and get stoned and watch the movies; in the evening we'd go to somebody's apartment and play records, and later we'd go uptown to all-night jam sessions." A hero of his was Milt Gabler, who ran his own label, Commodore, and paid with his own bread to record Billie Holiday, Jimmy Yancey, Meade Lux Lewis, Art Hodes, and James P. Johnson.

What kind of way of life was that, for somebody whose mother had hopes her son would be a writer? "She used to shut me in my room with sheets of yellow paper so I could write the Great American Novel."

Jerry finally got serious about writing when he was drafted, because it meant he could stay as far away as possible from any battles—"I had no Mailer complex about getting involved in the fighting"—and when the war finished he went back to Kansas State and finished his degree, in journalism. When he graduated from Kansas State, jobs were hard to find. Life was tough, especially as Jerry was supposed to be supporting his wife Shirley, whom he'd married in 1941. After some scuffling he got a job writing biographies of contemporary music stars like Perez Prado for Russ Sanjek at BMI. Sanjek passed the bios on to radio announcers for use as continuity aids. But after a few months of writing, Jerry fell sick and lost the job.

"We were living in one room at my mother-in-law's house, and I couldn't get a break anywhere, and then Meyer Shapiro, the PR man at BMI, heard there was an opening at *Billboard,* sent me over there, and Joe Csida hired me. I knew nothing about the commerical music business—I was a purist jazz fan, right?—and they sent me out on stories. But the thing they liked was that I knew how to put a sentence together, with paragraphs, and even knew how to use semicolons.

"I was there about four years, and I used to do something they don't do anymore. Every day, as soon as I'd got to the office, I'd get out there and use shank's mare, I'd go to the top of the Brill Building and work my way all the way down." The Brill Building at one-six-one-nine Broadway, housed the offices of many music publishers, record companies, management agencies, and PR firms, and was the hub of the music business.

"But then the editor, Joe Csida, who was a very opportunistic man, ordered me to go and compile a dossier on the Weavers—this was the McCarthy era. Well I was friendly with the Weavers, and anyway it was against my principles, so I told him there was no way and as soon as I could I left *Billboard*."

But this time Jerry had a job waiting. Howie Richmond, who was PR man for the Big Three publishers (Robbins, Feist, and Miller), was planning to start his own firm. So he arranged to have Jerry take over his own job until he got his own company rolling. Howie "got me hired as his replacement, with the idea that as soon as he built his company up a bit, he'd bring me into it. And he did build up a great catalogue, starting with the Weavers' material and winding up with the huge Richmond Organization that exists today."

Howie Richmond was picked out for special comment in an article on Tin Pan Alley in *Esquire* (February 1952), for employing "ingenuity and honesty" in a business that "has always been characterized by a certain amount of fraudulence." Jerry certainly picked up some of Howie's traits, including a respect for the effectiveness and importance of the disc jockey in the music business. But he never did get to join Howie's new firm. Atlantic Records was on the horizon.

"I was very friendly with Ahmet and Herb, and in 1952 they asked me to come and work for Atlantic, to run the publishing company and have a piece of it. And I had the temerity to say no, I wanted to be in the records side, and I wanted a piece of that. They said no, they didn't think so, but it was all cool and we stayed friends. Then a year later, Herb was drafted into the army to do his service as a dentist, and they figured they needed somebody with a little business sense, who would come into the office in the morning and stay around all day, which Ahmet wasn't in the practice of doing. Ahmet would love to stay up all night, play around, do some recording sessions, come into the office around four or five in the afternoon; so somebody had to help out with the administration. So they let me buy some stock for a nominal amount, and I said sure, I'm set."

II

There were seventy releases on the Atlantic label from the time when Jerry joined the company in 1953 to the time when Herb came back in 1955, and thirty sides made the rhythm and blues top 10 chart in *Billboard,* apart from many more that sold very well. In the same period, the Cat subsidiary label had been formed and abandoned, after coming up with just one hit out of twenty releases, the pop-oriented "Sh-Boom." The newly formed Atco label had had nine issues without a hit during Jerry's first two years. Still, it was a good batting average, thirty-one big hits out of 100 releases, especially at a time when competition was growing stronger. Independent record companies were waking up to their potential. No longer content to concentrate on the local market and enjoy occasional hits that broke out nationwide, indies now tried to establish themselves as national companies.

A relative novice to recording studios, Jerry was valued most at the start for promotion. He was the man who went on the road to meet disc jockeys around the country

Joe Turner (right) checks the pressings of his latest release, with Ahmet and Jerry.

and then maintained contact—and pressure—with regular calls from the office, now based at 234 West 56th Street. Of course, Ahmet and Herb had laid a solid background for him. They had "institutionalized" one major trip to the South each year, a custom that would be maintained. On one of his first trips, Ahmet had learned how some other companies worked:

"One of the first times I went into a radio station to ask them to play my records, there were two cats already there—Irving Katz and Bobby Shad. [Katz was promotion man for Apollo and Shad owned Sittin' In With.] The station had all its seventy-eights in a library, and we were waiting in there, and there was nobody from the station around. So Bobby says, 'You wanna see how to promote? What's the name of your label?' I told him Atlantic. So he said, 'Well you're over there, near Apollo, which is Irving's label. And my label, Sittin' In With, is here.' Then he took a big key and ran it along the rows of the rest of the records. He said, 'It cracks the records. So then they gotta play yours, right?' "

Ahmet and Herb learned fast enough, although that wasn't quite their style. They couldn't hope to cover the whole country themselves, plugging Atlantic's latest releases and keeping on top of what was selling, so they made reciprocal arrangements with the owners of companies in other parts of the country. Ahmet would tell New York stations about records on Specialty, Modern, and Chess, while Art Rupe, the Biharis, and Leonard Chess would push Atlantic records in their areas. But of course nobody was ever sure if the other guy was fulfilling his part of the bargain. So Ahmet once had a word with Leonard about it. Ahmet asked: " 'How come you're not promoting Atlantic records in Chicago anymore?' He said, 'What do you mean? I am promoting them.' I said, 'No, not really promoting them, not the way we've been promoting yours over here.' He said, 'What do you mean?' I said, 'Man, I'm really doing a job on your records. We were driving through Atlanta the other day, and we tuned into this station, and I heard them playing King records, and Atlantic records, and Exclusive records, they were playing every kind of record except Chess records. So I stopped the car at the next phone booth, and I called up the station, and I said let me speak to the disc jockey. They said who's speaking, and I said never mind who's speaking, get me that jockey. So somebody comes on and said this is the disc jockey, and I said listen motherfucker, this is Chess Records. Have you got a wife and family? You want 'em to live? Well you better start playin' our records.' I said to Leonard, 'That's what I call promoting records. Now, what are you doing for Atlantic in Chicago?' "

And the terrifying thing about the story, for Leonard Chess, was in not knowing where the joke was, because Ahmet's behavior toward the disc jockey wasn't far removed from the image that Chess Records already had in the business. Ahmet was quite capable of actually pulling a stunt like that, but would get equal enjoyment out of tormenting Leonard with the idea that he might have pulled it.

Sometimes the inter-indie competition involved the music itself. On one of the first trips South after Jerry joined Atlantic, they paid a visit on Dewey Phllips, by far the most important disc jockey in Memphis, and a legend in pop music mythology since he played Elvis Presley's first record seven times in one night soon after it was issued in the spring of 1954. The custom was for record company representatives to drop by during his show, give him some cash in appreciation of his good work (and conceivably in the hope that he might play a company record or two while they were there). Ahmet and Jerry followed custom to the tee, but they'd mistimed their visit, as Dewey delightedly told his audience over the air.

"I got these two crooks here from New York City, from

Atlantic Records. They're in town, but we know it's no use, don't we folks, because Leonard Chess has been here and gone." And had left Dewey with enough cash in his pocket to taunt these two and the gifts they brought. Still, Jerry was quite taken by Dewey's approach to his job.

"We were standing at the back of the booth behind him, and he was shouting, 'How you doin' all you Memphis chicks . . . and motherfuckers?' but he'd closed the mike off for the last part."

At any rate, after the show, Dewey took them down to a Memphis bar to meet Elvis. It was 1954, and Atlantic was hot on Elvis' trail, partly because Paul Ackerman, *Billboard's* music editor and Jerry's former boss, was excited by Presley's first Sun single, which wasn't widely known then. Ahmet says he was prepared to pay as much as $25,000 to Sam Phillips of Sun for Presley's contract, but RCA-Victor stepped in with a better offer. Jerry recalls waiting for Elvis with Dewey Phillips:

"After the show he took us down to a bar to meet Elvis in a little after-hours club next to the Home of the Blues, Ruben Cherry's record store. When we got there, Elvis isn't around yet, so we sit at the bar and get the booze, and Ahmet says, 'So Leonard Chess was here, huh?' and Dewey says, 'Yeah.' Ahmet says, 'What's his new record?' Dewey says, 'Hootchy Cootchy Man.' So Ahmet sings, the whole thing, all the words. Dewey nearly fell off his stool, and from then on we were buddies."

Ahmet takes up the story. "Yeah, being buddies meant that the next time we went to Memphis, and we go into the radio station to meet Dewey, he has lined up a pint of bourbon, and he says I have these fantastic chicks coming in, and we say, yeah? And then seven or eight girls aged between twelve and fourteen, pimply, dirty-looking, horrible little chicks come in, you know, like those little girls you sometimes see with sailors, wearing sockettes and high heels?

"So Dewey gave them a bottle of bourbon, and I can see Jerry looking very worried, like, oh my God, these chicks are about the age of my daughter, suppose I get arrested? Then Dewey says, 'Some of my friends are coming up later,' and these guys come in, about six feet, eight inches tall, and Dewey says, 'I want you to meet these guys, they're from Memphis State College and they're going to play basketball in New York next week.' He said, 'I thought we'd go and play some basketball a little later, after the show.'

"So I thought, oh my God, and Jerry says, 'I don't think we'll do that,' but Dewey won't listen, and we pile downstairs, with Dewey and these giants and their midget chicks, and we drive over to the campus, where the basketball gym is locked up, it's three o'clock in the morning, right? But the guys bust the door open, switch the lights on, get the baskets and balls out, and start playing. So there's Jerry and me, sitting on the sidelines with these little chicks. So Dewey, the idiot, goes up against one of the guys at the basket, falls down, and breaks his leg. So we go out and look for an ambulance.

"That's fun, right, selling records?"

III

One way or another, Atlantic did sell some records, having first taken the trouble to make sure that what they had was good. While they consolidated the careers of Ruth Brown, Joe Turner, and the Clovers, Ahmet and Jerry kept their eyes and ears open for undeveloped talent, and produced strings of hits with Clyde McPhatter, LaVern Baker, and Ray Charles. Atlantic's records before 1953 were aimed generally at the already committed audiences for black music, but now lyrics, choruses, and arrangements began to reach out for people accustomed to slighter "pop"

Success: Atlantic makes the front cover of Cash Box, *July 10, 1954. The caption reads: "Jerry Wexler, Ahmet Ertegun and Miriam Abramson, who run Atlantic records, sit before a gallery of their stars, all of whom won top Rhythm and Blues honors in* The Cash Box *Disk Jockey Poll. Ruth Brown was voted 'The Most Programmed Female Vocalist.' The Clovers were 'The Most Programmed Vocal Group.' The Drifters were named 'The Up and Coming Vocal Group.' And Joe Turner received two honors. His 'Honey Hush' was 'The Most Programmed Record' while he himself was voted 'The Most Programmed Male Vocalist.' Quite a lineup for one record firm."*

music. The documentary and recreative recording approaches gave way to a technique that could be called contrived or creative, depending on one's expectations of what a record should be. The producers believed they knew what would sell, and directed their sessions to achieve particular sounds and effects.

One of the first recording sessions supervised by the new combination of Ahmet and Jerry was the session with Clyde McPhatter and the Drifters that included their first hit, "Money Honey." The Drifters was a special project of Ahmet's, who more or less created the group.

"One of my favorite groups at the time was the Dominoes. I used to go and see them at the Apollo whenever they were there. Billy Ward had put them together, and he ran them like an army, they always looked great, slick. Billy was very well organized, the kind of guy who could have been running a successful record company."

The Dominoes were the most successful R and B vocal group in 1950 and 1951, when their Federal recordings "Sixty Minute Man" and "Have Mercy Baby" were huge sellers. In contrast to the "do-wah" sound of the Orioles and their followers, the Dominoes often recorded uptempo numbers and used professional-sounding harmonies. Clyde McPhatter's unorthodox, free-flying gospel voice wailed in the background on "Sixty Minute Man" and took the lead vocal on "Have Mercy."

"One night I went to Birdland, and Clyde wasn't there. I liked his high voice, and the way he sang, so I went backstage and said to Billy, 'Where's Clyde?' And he said, 'Oh, we fired him.' I said, 'Where is he?' And nobody knew, but he would probably be at home. So I found out his last name, got his phone number, called him up, had dinner the next day, and signed him up. He said he had some friends who would form a group, and he collected them together and brought them in for a session. We taped some stuff, but they weren't much good, not what I was looking for, which was a gospel sort of sound, which was how Clyde sang naturally.

"So he said he had another group of friends who were really good, gospel singers called the Thrasher Wonders, one of them could sound just like the bass of the Dominoes. I told Clyde he should change his name, Clyde McPhatter sounded like a Western comedy actor—Andy Devine or somebody—but Clyde liked his name."

The new formation, baritone Bill Pinkney and the brothers Andrew and Gerhart Thrasher, completed the lineup of Clyde McPhatter and the Drifters, and recorded Jesse Stone's "Money Honey." The lyric was comparable to a typical situation blues, but in a pop form with a sing-along chorus; it was sung with a gospel-styled inflection by Clyde, while the group chimed in with what Jerry called "bagpipe harmonies." Aah-ooh, aah-ooh. A year later, Hank Ballard and the Midnighters used the same sort of sound on several suggestive songs about a girl called Annie ("Work With Me, Annie," "Annie Had A Baby," recorded for Federal).

"Money Honey" was one of the biggest R and B hits of 1953. After that, each of the other five records by Clyde and the Drifters made the top 10 R and B list in *Billboard,* including the frantic "Such A Night," a near-calypso called "Honey Love," the enticing "Whatcha Gonna Do," and an extraordinary version of "White Christmas" which probably topped them all. The last three were cut at the same session, "Four sides in three hours," Jerry recalled, "And it was just a day's work. 'Whatcha Gonna Do' was written by Ahmet, and I think it is by far his greatest tune. 'The Twist' was outright stolen from it, and we could have sued, but we never liked to draw attention to ourselves as writers." Jerry rarely received credit as composer, but he was listed as co-writer, with Clyde, of "Honey Love."

Clyde brought his passionately intense and believable delivery to all of these songs, treating the composer's written melody as a rough guideline rather than a blueprint, yet never diverting from the expected in a studious, conscious way. The combination of an emotional tone with a creative melodic sense was almost unique, and although few of the compositions had much inherent lyrical quality, these records by the Drifters were probably the best that Clyde made.

But after only five or six sessions with the Drifters, Clyde was drafted. On his release from the service, he was persuaded by a wheeler-dealer manager, Irving Feld, to "go solo," leaving the name of the group to his former manager, George Treadwell. According to trade papers, Feld persuaded promoters to pay $3,500 a week for Clyde, which was certainly more than Treadwell had been able to negotiate for the Drifters.

The sound on "Money Honey" and "Such A Night" must have been particularly pleasing to Ahmet, as it represented the kind of sound he had been trying in vain to squeeze from the Clovers.

Buddy Bailey, the Clovers' lead singer, had much too mellow a voice to make the rough sounds Ahmet wanted. When Buddy was drafted, Ahmet brought in Charlie White, a singer with a raspier tone, to record with the Clovers, who maintained their string of hits with "Good Lovin'" (1952) and the double-sided hits "Little Mama"/"Lovey Dovey" (1953) and "Your Cash Ain't Nothin' But Trash"/"I Got My Eyes On You" (1954). When Bailey came back from the service to rejoin the Clovers, Charlie White was assigned to the Cat label with the Playboys, but neither of the group's two releases caused any stir, while the Clovers returned to softer songs, among which "Blue Velvet" and "Devil Or Angel" were good sellers.

Jesse Stone was responsible for rehearsing most of Atlantic's vocal groups before their recording sessions, in addition to providing musical arrangements for the sessions themselves. Not long after the Drifters had made their second record, the Chords walked into the Atlantic office with a song they'd written themselves, called "Sh-Boom." The lyric was as simple as vocal group songs tended to be: "Life could be a dream if I could take you up in paradise above," but the Chords sang it with such verve, Ahmet and Jerry decided to take a chance. They had Jesse rehearse the group and record it, and they issued it on the new subsidiary, Cat. The label was derived from "cat music," the regional name in Texas for the new music of the era which had not yet been universally christened "rock 'n' roll." The little chants of "sh-boom" by the group in the chorus gave the song a novelty appeal that distinguished it from other similar songs and it "went pop," making the national pop charts itself, although a cover version by the Crew Cuts for Mercury outsold it. Compared to contemporary R and B records, "Sh-Boom" had a quick, light beat, jaunty rather than aggressive, and the voices were soft, quite unlike the current sound of the Drifters and the Clovers. Still, the tenor sax solo, by Sam "the Man" Taylor, was quite tough. The pop market was definitely changing: this wasn't the first record by a black performer, recorded by an indie label, to find a wider market. "Gee," by the Crows, recorded for George Goldner's Rama label, had comparable success to "Sh-Boom" in 1954, and the previous year "Crying In The Chapel" by the Orioles, for Jerry Blaine's Jubilee label, had also done well in the pop market.

It's possible that if Atlantic had it to do over again, Ahmet and Jerry would have named their new label Rock & Roll Records instead of Cat. "Rock 'n' roll was the term used by disc jockey Alan Freed, a recent arrival to New York whom Jerry did not take to his heart. So when given

Ruth Brown, in the studio with Jerry Wexler. She made a breakthrough for R&B singers in 1956 when she recorded some commercials for Lucky Strike cigarettes.

space in the July 1954 *Cashbox* to discuss the emergent trend in popular music, Jerry studiously avoided the term "rock 'n' roll" and plugged his own term, "cat music." Apart from misjudging the appeal of the expression, Jerry's piece was exceptionally foresighted in describing the emergent music revolution.

Jesse Stone was becoming known for his "commercial R and B" arrangements. While the other indies seemed to get pop hits by accident, Atlantic's records sounded as if they were deliberately intended to sound commercial. The customary rasps of black singers had been softened. The songs included sing-along choruses, and the beats were easy to dance to. In June 1954 Eddie Mesner, who owned the Aladdin label in Los Angeles, formed the aptly named subsidiary, Lamp, which was to be based in New York with Jesse Stone as its A and R director. The Regals, the Five Pearls, and the Cookies were assigned to the label. Although a few records were issued, none of them sold well enough to justify the cost of keeping up a New York office, so the label was abandoned and Atlantic took over the three groups, with no great success. The Cookies had been collected originally by Jesse as a female session group for backup vocals on other people's records, and after making three records under their own name for Atlantic, they joined the Ray Charles band as the Rae-lettes.

But of all the records that Jesse Stone was associated with, Joe Turner's "Shake, Rattle, and Roll" had the greatest and longest-lasting impact. It was recorded in February 1954, Joe's first session in New York for a year and a half, and the first that Jesse arranged. Apparently a spontaneous uptempo blues, "Shake, Rattle, and Roll" was a logical last step in a series of records that started with Joe's 1953 hit, "Honey Hush."

Although Joe's records had sold well during 1951 and 1952, he seems to have been a hard man to get into a studio. In May 1953 Ahmet suggested that Joe get himself into the studio nearest where he happened to be, which was New Orleans, and make a record that Atlantic could release. Cosimo Matassa engineered the session in New Orleans. Matassa's own studio, where the majority of New Orleans singers (including Fats Domino) recorded, was booked, so Joe's session took place in a radio station with music supplied by a band led by Pluma Davis. Only two songs were recorded, both written by Joe—"Honey Hush" and "Crawdad Hole." Both had a rough, undisciplined quality that was unusual for an Atlantic record, although it was perhaps as close as the label ever came to the rough but atmospheric sound of Amos Milburn that had inspired Ahmet to go South in the first place. "Honey Hush" became a hit, and encouraged Ahmet, now partnered by Jerry, to record Joe in yet another atmospheric guise; if Joe Turner the New Orleans singer could work, how about Joe Turner the Chicago singer? They arranged to have Elmore James play his whining, jangling guitar behind Joe and went to Chicago to supervise the session themselves. The result was the beautiful midtempo blues, "TV Mama," with another funny lyric by Joe and some very sensitive playing from Elmore.

Further encouraged, Ahmet and Jerry organized another New Orleans session, under their own supervision this time. Evidently impressed by the effect of a curious sawing trombone riff by Pluma Davis on "Honey Hush," they used one again on this song, "Midnight Cannonball," although here, with a different band, the riff sounded more obviously prearranged.

But although the record sounds good now, it evidently didn't seem strong enough at the time, for Atlantic held it back and called another session in New York, with Jesse Stone arranging. This time Jesse supplied the song himself, "Shake, Rattle, and Roll," under the nom de plume Charles Calhoun. Jesse wrote the song as Joe would have, as a combination of loose references and evocative descriptions: "You wear low dresses, the sun comes shinin' through. . . . You make me roll my eyes and then you make me grit my teeth." But where Joe was content with having conjured a specific impression, Jesse went a step further, to render the song into something with a recognizable shape and pattern, to give it "commercial appeal." Using an expression he heard at poker games, he wrote a chorus: "I said, shake, rattle, and roll [repeated three times]/You won't do nothing'/ to save your doggone soul." Sing-along blues.

The chorus was sung at the recording session by Jesse, Ahmet, and Jerry. The drummer played a socking offbeat,

After losing the fight with Georgia Gibb's cover version of "Tweedle Dee," LaVern Baker (above, and right) was featured in the film Rock Rock Rock and broke through to the pop charts in '57 with "Jim Dandy"; still in their teens, the Bobettes (top right) had their one big hit the same year with "Mr Lee."

and Van Walls ran a marvelous, rippling boogie piano through it all. The record became a big R and B hit, and a white rock 'n' roll outfit called Bill Haley and the Comets covered the song for the pop market. Rock 'n' roll? What was that? A new music? Or a new label for a long-established music? Either or both, depending on what you'd been listening to up till then. For the R and B public, here was something just a little different from earlier hits by Amos Milburn and Ray Brown. The sound on Joe's records was cleaner, the beat was lighter, the accompaniment more polished. But still it was blues—or R and B—good dance music.

Not many people in the pop music audience heard Joe Turner's record, but more than a million bought Bill Haley's cover version on Decca. The lyric was changed so that all allusions to sex were dropped, and Bill's voice unmistakably belonged to a white singer. The novelty was in the pace and rhythm of the music, propelled by a stand-up bass and rim-shot drumming, punctuated by sax and guitar riffs. That beat, and the catchy chorus, were new to pop music, and justified the new label. And although Atlantic's record did not match the sales of the Decca cover, the publishing royalties did go to Atlantic.

IV

Even while he was putting rock 'n' roll together, Ahmet still found time to play his games; George Goldner took the brunt of a few of them. One of the leading New York record men, George started out recording Latin music on the Tico label, moved into R and B with the Rama label in 1953, subsequently formed Gee, Gone and End, and became a partner of Morris Levy at Roulette Records. Always receptive to new talent, he had no special flair in the recording studio but had a reputation as an exceptional promotion man. The music business is full of stories about promotion men who plugged the wrong side of a record and Jerry Wexler had one about George too.

One day Ahmet called up Goldner and somehow got straight through to his office without going through the switchboard. Goldner was on another line, to his distributor in Philadelphia. This was in the days before Gone and End, when George was running his Tico line, mostly mambo records, while his pop records were just a sideline, on Rama.

The distributor was ordering about forty different mambo records, two of this one, one of another, while Goldner took the order down himself. The distributor would ask for four of 867, seven of 868, two of 869 and so on. Ahmet wrote the order down too.

Goldner started asking the distributor to hurry it up, because he needed to take a leak. But the distributor continued being very discursive, and finally he got to a number and said, "Hey man, with this one, this Tito Puente record, you're plugging the wrong side," and Goldner said, "I don't wanna hear that shit, man, just finish the order off, I gotta take a piss."

Finally the order got done, and everyone hung up, including Ahmet. But then Ahmet re-placed the call, and when he got through to George he said, "This is Stanley Caldwell, I've got the big one-stop down here in Oklahoma City, and I wanna tell you, Mr. Goldner, that people down here aren't into Latin music, but since you started your lines, I'm pushing mambo real well."

And Goldner said, "Well that's fine, I'm glad to hear it."

But Ahmet said, "There's one thing, though, Mr. Goldner, I'm findin' it mighty hard gettin' your records."

So Goldner started motherfuckin' his distributor, and

Ahmet said, "Is there any way I could get your new releases?" Goldner said, "Sure, I'll take your order now, what do you want?"

So Ahmet started giving him the order, the same one he'd written down before: four of 867, seven of 868, two of 869. And Goldner, taking the order down, started muttering to himself, "Gee, this is real strange," and Ahmet said, "Excuse me, Mr. Goldner, would you mind taking the order down fast, 'cause I've got to go to the bathroom. Oh, but there's one thing, you know that new Tito Puente record? You're pushin' the wrong side." And Goldner started muttering again, and said, "Excuse me, Mr. Caldwell, but do you believe in providence?" He had no sense of humor, according to Jerry, if there ever was a Deadpan Daniel, Goldner was it. So Ahmet had to tell him. He said, "Come on, George. You know who this is." But George didn't get it, so Ahmet identified himself. And George said, "What are you doin' in Philadelphia?" Ahmet told him he wasn't in Philadelphia, but George figured he had to be to know what the Phillie distributor had ordered. So Ahmet got George to ring for Ahmet at the Atlantic number, to prove he was really in New York. And George wanted to know how Ahmet knew the Phillie distributor's order. So Ahmet said, "Goldner, you know you're always wondering how Atlantic stays so hot, keeps comin up with the hits. It's because we know everything everybody's doing, all the time."

V

It is curious and a little ironic that although Atlantic did a great deal to shape rock 'n' roll, they did not make a real breakthrough to the pop market in the years 1954–56 with a rock 'n' roll star in the way that their "friendly

Above: Ivory Joe Hunter signs with Atlantic in 1954, flanked by Jerry Wexler (left) and Ahmet Ertegun.
At right: Ivory Joe promotes his latest record. Joe's "Since I Met You Baby" was one of Atlantic's first pop hits, in 1956.

rivals" did: Lew Chudd at Imperial with Fats Domino, Leonard Chess with Chuck Berry, Art Rupe at Specialty with Little Richard, even George Goldner with Frankie Lymon and the Teenagers. One way or another, Atlantic's records were "too good."

The company had a consistent policy of nurturing real talent. As Jerry put it, "If a guy couldn't sing, we didn't sign him. And there were many nonsingers hitting in the rock 'n' roll period. That's why we had so few vocal groups. We had the best roster of singers of any company. We didn't go for the one-song, one-hit acts."

But if the company did go for people who were singers, they went for singers who did nothing else. Most of the independent companies recorded performers who supplied their own material and often their own accompaniments. Fats Domino wrote his own stuff and played piano; Chuck Berry wrote and played guitar. And in the previous generation, Charles Brown wrote some of his own material and played piano, while Roy Brown wrote virtually every record he made, although he didn't play an instrument.

Atlantic had resigned themselves to having to provide everything for the singer, for Ruth Brown, Joe Turner, Clyde McPhatter, the Clovers—and they applied the same technique to LaVern Baker and Ray Charles when they were signed up in 1952. Through Jesse Stone and other arrangers including Ernie Hayes and Howard Biggs, Atlantic evolved techniques for providing the best interpretations of various kinds of songs. And in the process, they unwittingly supplied musical models which other companies could follow.

The "cover" was the bane of the indies in this period. Major companies, with larger resources and wider distribution networks, could get their product to retail stores faster and in greater numbers than the indies could. Time and again, an indie would find a good song and a commercial arrangement, put out a record which started to sell, and then watch in frustration as a major copied their record and get most of the sales in the pop market. In 1954, Columbia's A and R director Mitch Miller was still looking for a song to follow Johnny Ray's extravagant "Cry," a hit three years before. Clyde McPhatter's interpretation of the Lincoln Chase song, "Such A Night," provided a suitable vehicle, and Johnny Ray had a chance of a hit again at last. But the powers-that-be decreed that "Such A Night" was not suitable for American airwaves, at least not when white people were known to be listening. In pop, young lovers were restricted to kissing, but the couple in "Such A Night" evidently hadn't stopped there.

Johnny Ray's "Such A Night" was unusual; cover versions of Atlantic records normally enjoyed a better fate. Mercury had special reason to be grateful for Atlantic's groundwork, for in addition to their hit version of "Sh-Boom" by the Crew Cuts, they successfully covered Ruth Brown's "Oh What A Dream" with a version by Patti Page, and LaVern Baker's "Tweedle Dee" with one by Georgia Gibbs.

Atlantic's arrangements were very "commercial" in the first place; the normal stridency and irregular melodies were restricted so that it became easy for the listening audience to sing along to the songs—a fundamental requirement of pop songs at the time, though not of rhythm and blues records. To emphasize this sing-along quality, Atlantic's records were provided with a male vocal chorus, the Cues.

Most of the records were cut in Atlantic's office with engineer Tom Dowd, the "kid" Ahmet had unwillingly accepted as a substitute back in 1948, now the regular first choice. Tom recalled: "Atlantic had an office in a loft on Fifty-sixth Street, it was a lovely address, two thirty-four West Fifty-sixth. That was their third office. There were two desks in the room, one for Ahmet and one for Herb—later used by Jerry when he joined. And there was

Tom Dowd, with and without beard. Tom's meticulous and sensitive engineering enhanced the sound of every Atlantic record and played a major role in keeping the company ahead of its rivals.

a miniature piano, so when people came to the office with a song, they could play it. And when it came time to record, they would pile one desk on top of the other, bring out some chairs for the band, and that's where Joe Turner recorded, Ray Charles, all those things in the early fifties."

Atlantic was famous for the clarity of its recordings, for which most credit is due to Tom; each instrument can be heard, and the level doesn't change during the instrumental solos, as it did on many of the more casually recorded records of the time.

It's possible that in making sure each instrument was properly heard, Tom lost a little of the "live," atmospheric sound that contributed to the excitement of records on Aladdin, Sun, and Chess. But Tom would probably prefer to compare his sound with what the major companies were doing in that period. "Sometimes we'd say, 'I want an RCA mix,' which referred to the effect that Victor—and Decca and Columbia—used to get when they would use just one or two microphones for the whole orchestral accompaniment, and push them way into the background so that there was just a sense of some sort of harmonic accompaniment, but all the focus was on the voice."

When one of the majors wanted a sound that matched the clarity of an Atlantic record, the best thing was simply to go for Tom. "Mercury . . . called me up after I'd engineered 'Tweedle Dee,' and said that they were going to cut the song again with Georgia Gibbs, and that they had the same musicians, the same arranger, and they wanted the same engineer."

VI

The Atlantic preference for "molding" its performers put LaVern Baker, Ruth Brown, and the Clovers ahead of other potentially comparable R and B performers in the competition for pop radio play and sales. Big Maybelle, for instance, was at least as good a singer as LaVern and Ruth, and she made some wonderful records for Columbia's R and B subsidiary, Okeh, using many of the musicians who worked on Atlantic session, including Sam Taylor and Mickey Baker. But Leroy Kirkland's tasteful and ingenious arrangements were firmly based in rhythm and blues conventions, and the records were "inaccessible" to the less sophisticated pop audience. But Atlantic's techniques almost foundered when they were applied to Ray Charles. Unlike Atlantic's other singers, Ray wrote his own material, played piano, devised arrangements; he couldn't so easily be persuaded to play what Atlantic A and R men thought would sell.

Originally from the Southeast—he grew up in Florida and Georgia—Ray started working professionally on the West Coast, and particularly in Seattle, Washington, in the years 1949 to 1952. Ray recorded more than sixty songs for various independent companies. At that time he sang and played piano in a style modeled closely on Charles Brown's. When one of his records, "Baby Let Me Hold Your Hand," became a national rhythm and blues hit in 1952, Ahmet and Herb recognized the Charles Brown influence and made enquiries about this new singer. It was found out that Swingtime, the company Ray was recording for, was in financial trouble and willing to let Ray go for $2,500. Atlantic paid the money.

They quickly appreciated that Ray Charles could do much more than imitate Charles Brown. People enjoyed the club blues sound on the West Coast, and Charles Brown was the best and most popular performer in the idiom, so it was natural that Ray had imitated him. But now the important thing was to make people realize that Ray was a versatile piano player and arranger who could play almost any kind of music.

The difficulty was to persuade Ray to get away from the old style. A session in September 1952 produced four jazz-influenced sides which were barely noticed when they were issued, and six months later another session was held, again in New York. Jesse Stone recalls that Ray was "very temperamental and hard to get along with, it was hard to persaude him to do the rock type things. But finally, after we'd done a few sessions the way he wanted to do them, he came into the studio and said, 'Okay, I'm not saying anything, you guys tell me what to do and I'll do it.' "

Ahmet wanted to hear him do some uptempo numbers, and since Ray couldn't or wouldn't write anything in this vein himself, Ahmet supplied a couple of songs; "Mess Around" and "Heartbreaker." A fascinating tape has been preserved of the rehearsals for these songs, with Ray playing a stomping piano while Ahmet teaches him the words by singing them. Occasionally, Ray breaks off into a dazzling thirty-second snatch of pure Bud Powell bop piano, or into a little Jimmy Yancey slow boogie.

But the song that finally broke the "new" Ray Charles to the R and B audience was a novelty jump blues, "It Should've Been Me," written by Memphis Curtis and sung by Ray in a slurred voice that parodied streetcorner cool. Its success evidently convinced Ray that he could be effective at faster tempos than he had been accustomed to, and he went on the road with a band to hone a new sound. By this time Jerry Wexler was with Atlantic; in a sleeve note on an album he recalled the next phase of Ray's career:

New Orleans—The First Arrangements

In December 1953, Ahmet and I were in New Orleans to record Joe Turner, then in full cry as a blues star. We ran into Ray at Cosimo's famous small studio, and Ray asked us please (!) to do a session with him and a pick-up band he was gigging around with in and around New Orleans. At this time Ray was close to Guitar Slim, the late blues singer from the bayou country, and was much taken with Slim's perfervid, impassioned, preach-blues style. Without portfolio, Ray had sketched out a head arrangement for Slim's *The Things I Used To Do,* playing piano at the date and directing things from the keyboard.

This record was to sell a million copies for the Specialty label. Nobody knew it then, but this was a big breakthrough for Ray—he had, in effect, written his first commercial hit arrangement.

Cosimo's was booked for the week, and we had to cut Ray in WSDU's radio studios. His band (pro tem, of course) was a group of erstwhile hard-boppers whose cards had been earned on the tin shed rhythm and blues one-nighter circuit. The great result was *Don't You Know.*

It was Ray's tune and arrangement, and while the side didn't upset the charts, it contained a memorable riff which may be heard any day you care to listen to various of our esteemed jazz groups, genus funk.

This was the landmark session in the growth pattern because it had: Ray Charles originals, Ray Charles arrangements, a Ray Charles band.

It was a non-A and R oriented date. Ahmet and I had nothing to do with the preparation, and all we could do at the session was see to it that the radio technician didn't erase the good takes during the playbacks.

The Gospel Style—The Sound is Fledged

In November of 1954, Ray called us to Atlanta to dig his new band. We got with him in the afternoon at the Peacock nightclub, where he had his band set to play for us. Except for Ray and his band, the place was empty, and as soon as we walked in Ray counted off and they hit into *I've Got a Woman* and that was it. Zenas Sears, now a successful radio station owner and operator and then an Atlanta deejay and buddy, got studio time for us in another radio station (more dues-paying time) and after much confusion we got out with a tape containing *I've Got a Woman, Greenbacks, Come Back Baby,* and *Blackjack* (during the session an announcer was doing a news broadcast from the control room and we couldn't play anything back).

But it had happened. Ray was full-fledged, ready for fame, and nothing basic has been really added since that day, just more of the same.

This was the sound: Ray sings and plays. The band lays out except for the rhythm section while Ray is singing a phrase. At the end of the phrase, Ray fills in on piano, like the great legendary guitar-playing blues singers or the piano blues men like Lloyd Gleen or Amos Milburn or Charles Brown. Here's the kicker: Ray's band doubles the piano figure, voiced to Ray's prescription. The band: two trumpets, baritone sax doubling on alto, tenor sax, drums, bass, piano, no guitar. *I've Got a Woman* was the archetype tune—16 bars, gospel chord progressions.

From then on Ray made a slew of hit records,

Three of the great singers of the late fifties, who each had big pop hits, 1958–9, but none was still with Atlantic by 1960; Chuck Willis (top) died after what should have been a minor operation in hospital, and both Clyde McPhatter (above, with the Drifters) and Ray Charles (right) moved on to other labels.

with songs he wrote and arrangements he dictated with that seven-piece band that was an extension of his own voice. Later came the Rae-lettes and strings, but the basics were there—especially the mining of the gospel lode that was to result in *Hallelujah I Love Her So, This Little Girl of Mine, Ain't That Love, Tell All the World About You,* and so many other marvelous originals.

Although it's true that Ray did write those songs, they were all secular transcriptions of familiar gospel songs; he was not a great lyricist, but used the accepted blues writer's technique of incorporating traditional couplets into new melodic contexts. Even as an interpretive singer, he was less truly creative than Clyde McPhatter; in a sense, he was now imitating a gospel singer—in particular, Alex Bradford—instead of imitating Charles Brown. He did not seem to have a personal style, but instead had a genius for absorbing and re-creating an entire sound. As Jerry Wexler wrote, his band sound was an extension of his vocal sound; at last Atlantic had a performer who was complete, self-sufficient. Once "It Should've Been Me" made the R and B top 10, most of his subsequent records were comparably successful. Unlike Atlantic's other hits, Ray's did not invite cover versions; it took a couple of years for session musicians to catch up with that kind of piano playing, those relaxed yet tight riffs. But despite the absence of competition, Ray's records didn't break through to the pop charts, not until 1957, when he spoon fed the audience by providing them with a song they already knew, "Swanee River Rock," as a way of making it easier for them to get used to his style. By then, Atlantic had got the knack of how to promote a pop record.

SEVEN:
DARIN', DRIFTIN',
COASTIN', AND GROWIN'

When Herb Abramson returned to the Atlantic office after two years in Germany, Jerry Wexler was in his seat and couldn't be moved. Herb had left Ahmet in charge of a small but prospering independent rhythm and blues record company, assisted by Herb's wife Miriam, who helped to keep the accounts straight and the bills paid, and by newly recruited Jerry Wexler, who had worked for the trade paper *Billboard* and for a music publisher but knew nothing about making records. When Herb came back from Germany two years later, Atlantic had continued its success as a rhythm and blues company and stood on the brink of the pop market. "Tweedle Dee," "Shake, Rattle, and Roll," "Such A Night," "Mambo Baby," "Oh What A Dream," and "Sh-Boom" had all been recorded first by Atlantic, built into R and B hits, and covered for the pop market by other, bigger companies, whose versions outsold Atlantic's. Any day now, Atlantic would get a record that was hard to cover, that got pop radio play and good distribution—and have a pop hit all to itself.

This change in Atlantic's status might have been okay for the returning Herb if it had not coincided almost exactly with Jerry Wexler's arrival and his own earlier departure. Jerry was sitting at Herb's desk and working beside Ahmet in the studios, and there was no easy way to push him out. Besides, Herb and Miriam had separated. Miriam was still working at Atlantic, so there were extra tensions. He was given an office of his own, and took over responsibility for the newly-created subsidiary label, Atco.

I

I arranged to meet Herb Abramson at 242 West 76th Street in what must have once been the banquet rooms of a hotel and were now the new, enlarged quarters of the A-1 Studio which Herb has owned and supervised for the past twelve years. As Herb later explained, there is a well-established tradition of locating recording studios in New York hotels because of the large space they offer for musicians, equipment, and offices. In contrast to some of the studios buried deep in the offices of large record companies, these independently run studios are more available and less expensive, allowing uncontracted artists to make inexpensive records or demos.

Although I made an appointment to talk to Herb here at this time, it's difficult to get him to relax and think back over long-forgotten events while tools clink and somewhere in the background a radio is playing today's hits today. Herb talks about some of the singers he's produced during the last ten years since he left Atlantic. Tommy Tucker, Titus Turner, Louisiana Red, rhythm and blues artists whose records have occasionally "crossed over" to a wider audience. Titus Turner wrote a number of intriguing songs with strange and memorable images, guaranteeing love "till the meat balls bounce" (in "Hold Your Loving") and "till grits ain't groceries, eggs ain't poultry, and Mona Lisa is a man" (in "All Around the World"). But Herb suggests we could talk at more leisure at his home. In this space, warmth, and comfort, the tape recorder no longer seems so nosy and Herb talks with enthusiasm about his life in the record business, consulting a scrapbook to check dates. But he recalls less about the period from 1956 to 1960.

When Herb came back from Germany, he took over complete responsibility for the newly formed Atco label, including signing new talent to the label, organizing the sessions, and overseeing promotion and distribution. It was Herb's chance to prove that he had not lost his touch, that Ahmet was mistaken if he thought Jerry Wexler was any kind of substitute as a producer. But competition was stiff. In the period following Herb's return, Ahmet and Jerry managed to redirect several rhythm and blues performers into the pop market, co-producing strings of hits for Clyde McPhatter, La Vern Baker, and the Drifters, signing up and getting pop hits for Ivory Joe Hunter and Chuck Willis, and finally breaking Ray Charles through to the pop market. They even got pop hits for veteran rhythm and blues singers Joe Turner, Ruth Brown, and the Clovers.

During all of this, Herb was not able to pick up where he had left off, although he did produce one hit for Clyde McPhatter, "Seven Days," and chose the material for another, "Treasure of Love." But other projects of Atco were more spectacular. First the Coasters and then Bobby

Darin, whom Herb had signed to Atco, proved that his distribution and his roster had potential. The Coasters were from the West Coast, a black vocal group put together by song writers Jerry Leiber and Mike Stoller to showcase their songs. They were signed to Atco as part of an unusual "independent production" contract between Atlantic and Leiber and Stoller which put the writers in complete control of the Coasters' recording career. In 1956, with both established rhythm and blues singers, including Wynonie Harris and Guitar Slim, and new singers including Bobby Darin, Atco had more hits than Atlantic. In 1957 Leiber and Stoller produced Atlantic's first million-selling record, the Coasters' double-sided hit, "Searchin' "/"Young Blood," on Atco.

Then, as Jerry Wexler recalls events, Ahmet by himself had signed Bobby after Don Kirschner persuaded them of Darin's potential as a singer-songwriter, assigning him to Atco. Herb supervised three unspectacular singles on the Atco label. Desperately anxious to have a hit and be famous, Bobby was particularly frustrated because Herb had temporarily delayed recording a novelty song that Bobby had written in conjunction with the mother of an upcoming New York dee jay, Murray Kauffman; the song was a novelty in the rock 'n' roll idiom called "Splish Splash." Bobby went into the other office and demonstrated the song to Ahmet and Jerry, explaining the Fats Domino type arrangement he envisaged. Jerry was not overly enthusiastic, but Ahmet liked the idea and agreed to allocate half of a forthcoming session to Bobby.

In an hour and a half, Bobby cut "Splish Splash," "Queen Of The Hop," and a couple more songs that served as B sides; both records were million sellers, a spectacular success for Ahmet in a period when he rarely went into the studio.

Complicating Herb's difficulties was the fact that his former wife Miriam still worked in Atlantic's office, which led to extra tensions between the staff there. Herb finally decided to ask the others to buy him out, and to use the money to start up on his own. He needed a fresh start.

While Herb had been in Germany, Ahmet's brother Nesuhi had come to New York from the West Coast to take charge of Atlantic's jazz catalogue and develop an LP department. Now Ahmet, Jerry, and Nesuhi raised $300,000 to buy up Herb's share of the company, and Herb ventured off on his own.

Even now, Herb concedes that the amount was fair, if not generous, and it certainly should have been enough to launch and sustain a viable record company. But the failure of the various labels he launched after breaking with Atlantic confirms the judgment of others working for Atlantic at the time that Herb was having a difficult period and that he may have misjudged the kinds of sounds that might be commercially successful or how much money needed to be spent on getting them.

Herb's labels included Triumph, Blaze, and Festival. He signed up Gene Pitney, Solomon Burke, Don Covay, and Bobby Comstock with an eye on the pop market, and recorded tapdancer Baby Lawrence, the comedians Butterbeans and Susie, and the jazz singer Eddie Jefferson for more specialist audiences. But not much worked out. Gene Pitney and Don Covay did eventually become very successful, but after they had left Herb; Solomon Burke wasn't eligible to record for him after all, as his contract with Apollo hadn't expired when Herb signed him. And when it did run out, Jerry Wexler signed him to Atlantic and had a long string of hits.

Bobby Comstock did have a hit, "Tennesee Waltz," which had an intriguing blend of biting blues guitar and shrill strings. But although Herb was on good terms with

Alan Freed (which Jerry Wexler was not), he had some distribution problems and subleased Bobby's next record "Jambalaya" to Atlantic. "They promoted it just enough to recoup the advance they paid to me, and then they let it die," maintains Herb. It's improbable that Atlantic would have wittingly let any record "die," even to spite Herb, though I sense Herb feels that any achievement of his represents a prick in the conscience of Ahmet and Jerry. But for the present Herb is secure, thanks to "Hi Heel Sneakers."

"Hi Heel Sneakers" was one of those unpredictable and unaccountable novelty hits that pop music throws up every now and then, not much different from any one of twenty-five boogie blues records in the same idiom by Jimmy Reed. Yet something in Tommy Tucker's original Checker version put it way up the charts and attracted countless subsequent recordings, including another hit version by Jose

Don Covay, an early protegé of Herb Abramson,
surfaced on Atlantic years later as a soul singer with
"Mercy Mercy" and "See Saw."

Feliciano. Herb Abramson produced the original Tucker master, which he leased to Chess, and he still owns the publishing rights.

However, Herb has projects for the future. He plays for me some tapes he has recorded of Louisiana Red, a blues singer with an unusually expressive voice. To my ears the unedited tapes lack direction and atmosphere. "I'm going to put out some blues albums—I think the market is ready, there are more people than ever before who're aware of the blues. I recorded an album by Elmore James for Fury, with Bobby Robinson, the one that's out in England on Blue Horizon."

(Eighteen months later, Atlantic issued an album by Louisiana Red, produced by Herb Abramson, which was gratefully welcomed by blues collectors.)

After I switch off the tape recorder, he relaxes and talks more freely for a couple of hours more, though I felt that a dissatisfaction with Atlantic flavors most of his comments. "They ought to have some kind of pension system for the people who made them what they are today, the singers like Clyde McPhatter—how do you think he feels, not being able to make a record? LaVern Baker, Ruth Brown, they put Atlantic at the top, and what do they get out of it? Jesse Stone." I wonder silently if Herb himself would have welcomed a share of Atlantic's success, but he does not suggest it.

When I see Jerry Wexler after my talk with Herb, he is anxious to know what Herb has to say, and seems relieved that so little was "revealed." "A pension system? That's a good idea. We ought to think about it."

II

Between the mid-1950s and the mid-1960s, Atlantic

evolved from a small record company which operated principally in the rhythm and blues market into a full-fledged popular music company, confronting its share of awkward moments along the way. Some of these were problems that face every "medium-sized" firm, some were personality conflicts within the company, and some related to the quality of the product being marketed. But Atlantic not only survived the transition, which scarcely any of the firm's rivals did, they managed to retain essentially the same decision-making executives operating with the same tenet: find a good performer and support him through thick and thin.

The problem with being medium-sized was that the firm was vulnerable from both below and above, from tiny companies and from the huge ones. It was still possible to launch a record company on a shoestring, starting with less than $1,000. Harry Weiss, one of the record men who testified before a congressional subcommittee investigating

---

Memo From Harry Weiss

Item	Amount
2,000 at 14 cents	$280.00
2,000 labels at $9 per thousand	18.00
4 sides mastering, at $11	44.00
4 strikeoff plates, at $15	60.00
Fare (air)	30.03
Taxis to and from airport	6.50
Taxis in New York City	4.50
Hotel	12.00
Per diem (food), 2 days	15.00
Total	470.00
Engineer at WORL	5.00
Total	475.00
Record promotion	175.00
Total	650.00

---

the business, supplied details of his operating costs for pressing and promoting 2,000 records (preceding page).

No office rent, no salaried staff, no warehouse costs, no advances to performers: a small firm had hardly any of the expenses of a firm such as Atlantic, whether or not it was currently enjoying a hit. In the case above, Harry Weiss doesn't seem to have paid any session musicians—evidently it cost him only a five-dollar fee to the engineer at WORL to record the song. The group being recorded must have supplied their own accompaniment free, hoping Harry would push their record and make them famous. If the record did become a hit, the group would then of course ask for better terms on the next record. At which point, according to the distorted budgeting system of most indie companies, it became more profitable to look around for another group than to pay this one high royalty rates.

Atlantic stayed loyal to their successful performers, not just because it was ethical, but because they found it was good business in the long run. If the quality of a particular singer's records was maintained, each hit was advance publicity for the follow-up; disc jockeys, distributors, record store owners, and customers became familiar with the singer's name.

This "marketing" concept was carried to its logical conclusion when Atlantic recorded a group previously known as the Five Crowns under the "trademark" of the Drifters. When Clyde McPhatter originally formed the Drifters, George Treadwell, then manager of Sarah Vaughan, became their manager and took out a copyright on their name. This copyright gave Treadwell the right to hire whomever he chose to be in the group. After Irving Feld persuaded Clyde to go solo, Treadwell brought in various singers to duplicate Clyde's sound. Although Clyde himself was still recording solo for Atlantic, Ahmet and Jerry duly recorded whoever came to the studio—and kept coming up with hits. But by 1958 Treadwell apparently got tired of holding the group together and abandoned it after the Drifters' hit, "Drip Drop."

According to Jerry, "More than a year went by after 'Drip Drop' and before 'There Goes My Baby' during which there were no Drifters and nobody made a move or gave a damn until it occurred to me to call George Treadwell and point out that we had a valuable property in the name, and to get a set of singers. In a matter of two or three months he came up with the Five Crowns with Benny King."

Jerry's term for this commitment to their artists is "valuable property." But sometimes the concept backfired, exposing Atlantic's vulnerability to big firms. In 1959, after a run of ten hits and some near misses on Atlantic and appearances in a couple of Hollywood "exploitation" movies, Clyde McPhatter signed with MGM. Less than six months later, Atlantic was even more stunned when Ray Charles moved to ABC-Paramount, just as he was finally breaking through to the pop market. "What'd I Say" had made the national top 10, and Atlantic had just recorded an album of "classy" arrangements, one side with strings and the other with a large horn section. In the last Atlantic sessions Ray recorded a song by the white country singer, Hank Snow, called "I'm Movin' On." After the move, ABC more or less duplicated the sessions, and made not only a succession of million-selling singles, but some million-selling albums, too.

All of which Atlantic probably could also have done if they had held onto the singer. Their problem was that although they could pay good royalty rates after sales, they didn't have the resources to make the payments in front, in advance. Which was how singers—and even more important, managers—liked to have it.

So Atlantic was in the precarious position of "breaking" a name to the general public, and then losing it to a bigger company. In the long run, the only answer was to become big enough to pay those big advances itself. Atlantic set out on this course and ten years later, the transformation was complete, as they outbid competitors for Aretha Franklin, the Rolling Stones, and others. But Atlantic had to beware of overexpansion. As Robert Townsend observed in *Up the Organization,* the tendency is for an ambitious small company to "look at General Motors and see finance committees, executive committees, planning departments, advertising departments, marketing departments, personnel departments, management development departments, and public relations departments, and say, 'Aha, so that's how they do it.' And a year later they're out of business. If you're a small or medium-sized business trying to make the grade, you're going to have to take on a few of the burdens of the publicly owned companies. But only a few. And for that reason carefully examine every new expense and activity to see whether it's a necessity or an ornament."

Veteran New York record man Hy Weiss, full of scorn for the inefficient and mismanaged big record companies that are able to absorb annual losses amounting to millions of dollars, likes the way Atlantic operates: "You walk into that office, and everyone's busy."

Jerry Wexler boasted: "I once hired a guy from Mercury, and he came to me after a week, he said this is not possible, it's not human to expect somebody to work like this. So he left us, and we still keep up the pace. Man, another company might have twenty people to work on liner notes for album sleeves. At Atlantic, that's just a part of one person's job. Nesuhi still reads proofs."

III

True enough, bustle characterizes the Atlantic office, which manages to cram into a couple of floors not only the promotion, press, and publicity staffs, but the recording studio and mixing rooms—and the offices of the executive vice-presidents. Nesuhi's office looks out over Broadway to Columbus Circle and a corner of Central Park. An array of LP sleeves on one wall reminds him of his latest product, but unlike practically every other record company, Atlantic doesn't adorn its offices with the self-congratulatory gold plaques that record companies like to buy to show off their million-dollar hits.

Nesuhi Ertegun joined Atlantic in 1955 and quickly set up an adventurous but self-sufficient jazz catalogue, adroitly financing experimental musicians including Ornette Coleman and John Coltrane with strong-selling combos like the Modern Jazz Quartet. Nesuhi had been even more passionately interested in jazz than Ahmet, Herb, and Jerry, and was probably the prime mover in initiating the Washington jazz concerts. Older than Ahmet, he was the first to begin collecting records, but was forced to abandon his first collection in Paris in 1939 when the war prevented his return from a holiday in the States to complete his Ph.D. in Philosophy at the Sorbonne. Stranded in Washington, his interest in jazz intensified.

"At about the same time as we started to stage jazz concerts in Washington, I began to lecture on jazz, at a place called the Book Shop. I gave a series of lectures on the history of jazz, playing records and talking about them. And one of the people I met through these lectures was Herb Abramson, who came to one of the lectures and stayed to talk about it afterward. I quickly realized that he knew more about jazz than anybody else in the room. And he offered to help us with any concerts we wanted to put on, because he knew a lot of the musicians in New York."

Toward the end of the war, Nesuhi made several trips to the West Coast, drawn by the double attraction of a

girl he was in love with, Marili Morden, and a lively
California revivalist movement for New Orleans jazz.
Marili owned a specialist record shop in Los Angeles, the
Jazzman Record Shop, and during his visits Nesuhi worked
there with her, learning a lot about the records by playing
them to customers every day. Within a few years, he was
in the business of making them.

"In forty-four, Orson Welles, who at that time had a
coast-to-coast radio show, called me and said, 'I'd like to
have a real New Orleans band on my show—could you
get one together for me?" So Marili and I said great,
here was a chance to get more exposure for the music
we loved, and we got a band together. Kid Ory hadn't
been playing recently, he was working in the post office,
but we persuaded him to make a comeback. And we got
the clarinettist Jimmy Noone, who was playing with his
group on Hollywood Boulevard. He was one of the most
musical guys I ever met; you get no idea of his depth
from listening to his records. Mutt Carey, trumpet, had
been working as a porter on the railroads; he said he'd
try. Zutty Singleton, on drums, was already living in Los
Angeles, and he's to this day one of my closest friends.
Ed Garland, the bass player, could do it.

"So I called Orson up and said I've got the band together,
and he said great, bring them over to the studio to rehearse.
So we went over to the CBS studios. Some of those guys
hadn't seen each other since 1918, since they'd all been
in New Orleans. They all fell into each other's arms, and
then they said, what'll we play? How about "High Society"? So Noone goes into that chorus solo, and they play
a little, and then the big man, Welles, comes into the
studio, and I take him around to each of the guys in the
band and introduce him. We got to Kid Ory, and I said,
'This is Kid Ory; Ed this is Orson Welles.' And Kid looked
at Welles, and said to me, 'What was that name again?'

When Ahmet's brother Nesuhi joined Atlantic, the company signed up a slew of major jazz figures, many of them managed by Monte Kay, including the Modern Jazz Quartet (left) and the Jazz Workshop, led by bassist Charlie Mingus (right). Over the years, jazz played an important role in providing Atlantic with "catalogue" product that sold consistently over the years. But although that label once made a point of signing innovators like Mingus, Ornette Coleman, and John Coltrane, there's been a conspicuous absence of avant garde jazz musicians on the label in recent years.

And I thought, oh no, this guy, he has a tremendous ego, he's going to throw us all out, and I said, very clearly, 'Orson Welles,' and he says, 'Oh yeah, sure, I heard of you.' And Orson was great, he liked the band, and he fixed for them to go on the show. And for some reason they scored a triumph, mail started to pour in, and Orson Welles said, 'I want to keep them on'—he had about thirteen weeks to go—he said, 'Can you arrange it?' I said sure.

"So they played three weeks, and a couple of days before they were due to do the fourth week, Jimmy Noone came around to see me, to discuss a plan we had for him to record, not with this exact group, but along those lines. He was with me for about two hours, went home, and the next morning, shaving in his bathroom, he died. April 1944.

"So I called up Orson Welles and told him he couldn't have a band for the show tonight, because Jimmy Noone had died. But he called me back a little later, and said tonight I want to do a tribute to Jimmy Noone: find another clarinet player, bring the band, and we'll do something. So I called in Wade Wailey, a player of much less ability than Jimmy, but the best I could find that day.

"Of course the band was very depressed, but Orson Welles came and said tell me all you know about Jimmy Noone. So I told him what I knew, where he was born, how he started, who he played with, that kind of thing; he didn't take any notes, just listened. And that night he went on the air, with no script, and he talked about Jimmy Noone, and it was one of the most moving things I ever heard in my life. And when he finished, I was in tears, the band was in tears, and he said, 'Now we're going to play the blues, for Jimmy.' And the band played beautifully."

When Nesuhi's father died in 1946, Nesuhi decided to marry Marili and move permanently to Los Angeles. For the next few years he worked at the Jazzman Record Shop and for some of that period edited *Record Changer* as an unpaid hobby.

For a while Nesuhi also ran his own label, called Crescent after New Orleans—"The Crescent City"—and the design on the Turkish flag. On this label he recorded sixteen sides by the Kid Ory band. But gradually Nesuhi's taste was changing from a purist passion for ragtime, early blues, and classic New Orleans jazz. At first dubious about the contemporary "bop" music of Dizzy Gillespie and Charlie Parker, he came to understand and like it, partly because he was exposed to it through the shop.

Nesuhi also gave the first course on the history of jazz at U.C.L.A. Introduced as an experiment, it was expected that maybe fifteen or twenty students might enroll; 120 signed up, and what had been started as a half-semester course ran on for four years, until Nesuhi went East to join Atlantic in 1955.

Around 1951, Nesuhi's marriage to Marili broke up. He left Jazzman and looked around for something else to do. A friend called Lester Keonig owned a moderately successful revivalist jazz label called Good Time Jazz, and invited Nesuhi to come to work for him; soon afterward, they started a subsidiary label, Contemporary Jazz, on which they recorded Barney Kessel, Shelley Manne, and other budding West Coast modern jazz men, on 33⅓ LP albums. But after three years he left to look for something else.

While changes in musical style were still almost imperceptible undercurrents during the late forties and early fifties, attention was directed to the "technological" revolution sponsored by major companies RCA and Columbia. RCA was determined to make the old breakable 78s redundant by introducing the 33⅓ LP unbreakable album, while Columbia sponsored the single-play seven-inch 45. The shift to these new configurations was an expense the indies would rather have avoided, but by the mid-fifties there was no choice. Even relatively poor record buyers had bought equipment that played the new records.

In 1955 Lew Chudd, owner of Imperial, was planning to move into the growing album field, and made an attractive offer to Nesuhi of partnership in an LP line, with responsibility for supervising compilations and packaging. It sounded good to Nesuhi, so he called Ahmet up in New York to tell him his plans.

"Ahmet said, 'Oh no, you can't do that. Atlantic is going into LPs too, and you're supposed to be an LP specialist; come and do it with us.' I said no, I liked living on the West Coast. I had friends there. I didn't want to move to New York. But he talked me into it." They discussed setting up a West Coast branch, but Atlantic couldn't afford two separate offices, so Nesuhi agreed to go in with them in New York. For the first year or two he lived six months on the West Coast and six months in New York.

Part of Nesuhi's role was to compile LPs from Atlantic's catalogue of single-play 78s and 45s, but he also began to sign up jazz singers and musicians whose work was recorded specifically for release on albums.

Largely through Herb and Tom Dowd, Atlantic had been involved in new sound ideas, especially stereo, and before Nesuhi joined Atlantic, it had recorded the first stereo album, called binaural then, a Wilbur De Paris Dixieland jazz album. The record had to be played on special equipment with two needles, which very few people had.

"We decided to record everything in stereo long before there was a general market for stereo records. Tommy set up both systems so he could record everything in both mono and stereo. When I went out to record in California, I used to *carry* stereo equipment on the plane with me, just so we had stereo tapes of what we did. The regular engineer would record in mono, and I would hire another engineer to be in the studio with this portable stereo equipment to take the stereo version. We felt that stereo was the coming thing, and that if our records were to have a lifespan of more than a year, we needed to have them ready for the new system."

Within a couple of years, Atlantic became a leader among the handful of independent companies recording the best modern jazz musicians, having been given a good start through Nesuhi's connections in California.

"The first people I recorded were my West Coast buddies, Shorty Rogers, Jimmy Giuffre, Shelley Manne; they all wanted to record for me at Atlantic. But our biggest break was signing the Modern Jazz Quartet, who were at that time probably the biggest jazz group in the world; their contract with Prestige had run out, and every label was trying to sign them. But they were very choosey with whom they would go, and under what conditions; their manager was Monte Kay, who also handled Charlie Mingus and one of the best jazz singers, Chris Connor. And we signed all of them at the same time, making unusually high advances per album for that time. In those days, it was a big coup for us to get those musicians. Chris Connor was a very big name; she'd just left the Stan Kenton Orchestra.

"But the strangest experience was signing Lennie Tristano. I always thought he was a fantastic musician—he's a pianist and composer—but I'd never met him. I called him and said I'd like to record him for Atlantic, so he invited me to come to his house to talk about it ."

Never widely known outside jazz circles, Tristano was respected among expert fans as being one of the most adventurous and truly progressive experimental musicians of the fifties.

"So I went to see him; this was fifty-five or fifty-six,

and he wanted to know why I thought I was qualified
to record him. It was really like a test; he wanted to make
sure he would be in the right hands. He played me records
and asked me my opinion—some of them he thought were
good and some very bad, and he wanted to know my reac-
tions. And of course I couldn't tell if I was giving the
right answers.

"After about an hour I was leaving, and I noticed an
abstract sculpture near the door. Lennie's blind, totally
blind, but he sensed me stop next to the sculpture and
he said, 'Who is that?' So I looked at it, and there must
have been something there, and I said, 'That's Charlie
Parker.' And he said, 'I record for you.' I'd passed the
test."

Nesuhi also supervised some Ray Charles albums. He
persuaded jazz promoter George Wein to put Ray on at
the Newport Jazz Festival and had Tom Dowd record it.
He also worked with Jerry Wexler on a special double
session that became the album *The Genius of Ray Charles*.

"We decided to make one side with strings and one side
with a jazz band. I thought that to get the two best arrangers
of the time, we needed Quincy Jones to do the jazz band
side, and Ralph Burns to do the strings side. We did several
rehearsals with Ray and Ralph Burns, but it was harder
to get Quincy in, because Quincy, whom I love, is a little
disorganized; he very often takes on more than he can
handle.

"There was no problem with Ralph Burns at all, everything was done, we got some very good sides. For the
jazz band sides we were going to record on a Sunday afternoon, and I got a band together that you wouldn't believe.
I had most of the Basie band, five guys out of Duke Ellington's band, Ray's own band, and the girls for the vocals.
Thirty-five people, something like that. We'd carefully chosen the songs, all we needed was Quincy's arrangements.

"Sunday morning, about eight o'clock, I get a call from Quincy Jones. I say, 'What's the matter?' He says, 'I'm not ready.' I said, 'What do you mean?' He said, 'I don't have the arrangements ready.' I said, 'We've hired all these musicians, we've booked the studio, we have to record this afternoon.' He said, 'Man, I'm sorry, I've let you down, forgive me . . . but I'm, not ready.' I said, 'Do you have *any*thing ready?' He said, 'Yeah, I did one number.' He was supposed to write six. He said, 'I can finish one.'

"Catastrophe, right? I said, 'Quincy, you finish that one, ok?' He was suddenly relieved: 'One I can do, I swear to you.' I said, 'Okay, now you know what the tunes are, and you have the keys they're in. Here are some phone numbers, I want you to call each of these guys and give them a song to do, by this afternoon.' He said, 'Do you think they can do it?' I said, 'It'll work,' and I gave him the phone numbers; I forget now who they were—Al Cohn, Ernie Wilkins. I said, 'If they're in town, they'll do it. They're friends of mine.' I think Ralph Burns did one for that side too, which he wasn't supposed to have to do.

"And that afternoon we had a scene in the studio. Because although each guy had written the arrangements, they had to be copied for all those instruments, one for each man, right? So there were desks and copiers all over the studio desperately finishing one song as we played the one before. We had booked a double session to do the six sides—three hours, then a break, then another three hours. And we finished ahead of time. And you listen to that beautiful record and you can't believe the conditions under which it was made.

"In the middle of one of the numbers, the band was blasting, and Ray stopped. I said, 'What's the matter?' He said, 'One of those trumpets, I think it was the third, played a wrong note.' I told the arranger, who said he hadn't heard it. But we had the trumpets play their parts, softly, with no rhythm section, and sure enough one of them had a wrong note there—probably copied down wrong. Ray had such an understanding of music, I'd never seen anything like it. He would be making changes all the time, dictating all the chord changes, everything that was needed to incorporate his suggestion. A complete musician."

For six or seven years Atlantic was known as a company that would record "the latest" in jazz. Nesuhi heard the Ornette Coleman group (with Don Cherry on trumpet, Charlie Haden on bass, and Ed Blackwell on drums) in a garage in Los Angeles and was impressed. "Ornette has a lot of basic jazz and blues in his playing, and the rest is himself. I don't think he takes much from European music, the source of many avant garde musicians." After one LP on Contemporary, Ornette moved East and recorded for Atlantic until ABC signed him in the early sixties. Charlie Mingus and John Coltrane also made some important innovative records for Atlantic, but since ABC signed Coleman and Coltrane to its Impulse jazz label in 1962, Atlantic seemed to lose interest in nurturing experimental but expensive jazzmen and more or less abandoned the frontiers of modern jazz. Instead, much of Atlantic's current "jazz" catalogue sounds like hip muzak, played well and fashionably to back up conversations at parties. Nesuhi explains that he doesn't like most avant garde jazz, "And I think it is important to record music you like. I do like Eddie Harris, Les McCann, Herbie Mann, and we record them."

Nesuhi also likes the piano player Thelonius Monk, and once made a record with him—a noncontract one-shot deal where he put Monk and the Art Blakey band together for an album of all original Monk compositions. Ever since he played in the legendary wartime "be-bop" after-hours sessions in Harlem with Charlie Parker, Monk had been among the most admired avant garde jazz musicians, and had also developed a reputation for bizarre eccentricities outside the studios. For several years, he kept company with a lady of aristocratic bearing who was known as the Baroness. By comparison, Art Blakey was socially conventional, although as a drummer he contributed a lot to the new style, flurry-of-noise technique of rhythmic accompaniment which is now standard in modern jazz.

"I decided to record them at the Capitol studio on Forty-sixth Street. They all came late the first night, which was usual, but finally they did all come, with a lot of other people, the Baroness was with Monk, everybody was with somebody, I didn't mind.

"When they sat down to play, the Blakey musicians found it very difficult to deal with Monk's music; there were a lot of rhythmic accents in strange places that you didn't notice until you tried to play with him. And after an hour or so, I said to Monk, 'Don't you have any lead sheets or anything, that the musicians could read, to get a sense of what the compositions were?' He said, 'Yeah, I've got lead sheets.' I said, 'Where?' He said, 'In my briefcase.' I said, 'Well, get them out.' He said no. I told Art, 'Monk's got the music in his briefcase.' Art said, 'Monk, you got the music?' He said yeah. Art said, 'Well give it to the guys.' Monk said, 'No, they have to learn, without seeing any music; that's the way they'll really learn.'

"Which is true, if they really have time to rehearse. I'll never forget what Blakey said. He said, 'Monk, you're a genius. These guys are just musicians, and they'll kill themselves for you—but help them, show them the music, even if they have to put it back after they've looked at it.' No. And he never did take out the music.

"They worked for four or five hours, and nothing was happening. They weren't getting together at all. The atmosphere wasn't cordial. The bass player passed out, just slid along the floor. Blakey looked across at somebody else in the room and said, 'That guy can play bass.' And he turned out to be somebody very good. But at one o'clock in the morning, the tape recorder hadn't even been started, they hadn't done anything, and it was time to finish. And I said, 'Okay, we'll meet at the same time tomorrow night.'

"Blakey's manager looked at me. He said, 'Man, you're a gambler, you're a sport, you wanna try this again?' I said yeah, because I thought there was something potentially there. And sure enough, when they started the next day, something did start to happen, but in a very strange way. Monk would play a fantastic chorus, and then he'd get up, and waltz around the room with the Baroness. I was afraid he would bump into a mike, but he didn't; he was in a good mood. In the last hour and a half, after all the confusion, it began to click, and we could record.

"Finally, in spite of all the odds, we made what I think is a very good jazz album, and the band left. I stayed another half hour or so listening to playbacks, and then I went out. And there was a scene. It was almost dawn and there were Monk and the Baroness in her Rolls Royce, and the Blakey band, who had worked so hard all those hours, Johnny Griffin, Bill Hartman, great musicians who had worked so hard to play Monk's music the way he wanted, here they all were, dead and exhausted, trying to push the huge car to get it started because its battery was dead."

Nesuhi believed the role of the producer in jazz was always to supervise, not to create; the artist always has the last word. "I'll make my two cents' worth of suggestions, but it's up to the artist to take or leave my advice. For them, a record is a very important thing. It's what they are leaving to posterity, and it has to be what they feel they want at that moment. What we did with Coltrane, Mingus, Ornette, was what they wanted to do at the time. And we train our producers to work this way. We're glad if the artist wants to be present at the mixing sessions, and the editing, because it's his work we're dealing with."

Nesuhi gave no hint of the frustrations he must have endured when musicians had insisted on keeping in passages which sounded redundant to the producer, but did recall with awe the malleability of singers at one of the rare pop sessions he supervised.

Very soon after he joined Atlantic, and while he was still on the West Coast, Nesuhi was asked to supervise a session by the Drifters. "They had a new lead singer [Johnny Moore], and I was really just guessing because I had no experience with this kind of music. But we did five songs and each one of them became a chart hit. I was surprised with their flexibility; compared to a jazz group, you can do so much more with them. You could accomplish so much by changing things, whereas in jazz it all depends on the inspiration of the guy on the day. He has it, or he doesn't, and you are at the mercy of his mood."

IV

The jazz and album catalogue provided a regular, reliable income for Atlantic, but singles continued to be the main source of earnings until the late 1960s. For a while Atlantic depended heavily on the production team of Leiber and Stoller, whose output increased as Ahmet and Jerry's involvement in studio production declined. Ahmet's solo production of Bobby Darin's "Splish Splash" came near the end of a fairly close Ertegun-Wexler studio relationship, and from 1958 their roles tended to become more distinct. Ahmet and Jerry worked together with Clyde McPhatter and Ray Charles until they left the company, and with Chuck Willis until he died, but they passed Ruth Brown, LaVern Baker, and the Drifters over to Leiber and Stoller.

Ahmet also continued to produce Bobby Darin after "Splish Splash," but before "Queen Of The Hop," which was recorded at the same session, could be issued as a follow-up, complications developed. A record appeared on the Brunswick label called "Early In The Morning" by a group named the Ding Dongs, whose lead singer sounded remarkably like Bobby Darin. Investigation revealed that in his period of frustration with his slow start at Atco, and anticipating that his contract would not be renewed, Bobby had done a recording session for the Decca subsidiary, Brunswick, under the supervision of Murray Kauffman. Out of this session came the gospel-styled chant which sounded like a potential hit. Undeterred by the fact that Bobby was kept on at Atco, Brunswick had issued the record anyway. Atlantic retrieved "Early In The Morning" and reissued it on Atco under the name of the Rinky Dinks, while Decca met their outstanding orders for the song by rushing Buddy Holly into the studio to re-record the song. Darin's version was the bigger hit, because his voice and delivery were better suited to the Ray Charles idiom in which Bobby had written the song.

"Queen of the Hop," which was sung in the same Fats Domino idiom as "Splish Splash" had been, was belatedly issued and duly made the top 10, but subsequently Bobby Darin started veering toward a classier sound. He used strings and voices instead of a sax section on "Dream Lover," and so craftily disguised the typical "teen-beat" chord progression of the era. "I had just discovered the C-Am-F-G_7 progression on the piano," he told a radio interviewer later. "I stretched them out and I liked the space I felt in there, and the words just flowed. I felt it should have voices and strings, so it was a bigger date than I'd been used to. We did thirty-two takes on the song, because we couldn't get everything to jell. But it was well produced."

Bobby soon became an institution on pop radio, translating standards into youthful, hip ballads with a beat. "Mack The Knife," "Beyond The Sea," "Lazy River," "You Must Have Been A Beautiful Baby" were among the twenty hits he recorded for Atco before he was lured to Capitol in 1962, presumably as a replacement for Frank Sinatra, who had left Capitol to form his own company, Reprise.

Bobby Darin was among the many Italian-American singers who "rescued" popular music from the rhythm and blues and white southern singers who had threatened to change its character with rock 'n' roll, but Atlantic exercised commendable restraint in refusing to jump on the teen idol bandwagon they helped to set rolling. The main criticism that could be made of Atlantic's records in the late fifties was that they tended to submerge the character of their good singers—LaVern Baker, Chuck Willis, Clyde McPhatter—in stereotyped vocal group choruses, which may have been effective in getting the singers into the charts, but which make the records hard to endure now. Responding to a criticism along these lines, Jerry Wexler replied in a letter:

"As for those vocal groups we used in there behind LaVern and Chuck, I could kick my ass every time I hear those tunes; attribute it to insecurity and fright, trying to survive in the land of the Hilltoppers and Pat Boone. What did we know? All I can say is that a hell of a lot of our records sound terrific today; they are in tune, and you can hear the bass! Compared to some of the a capella crap that hit around the same time, our stuff sounds incredible.

"Remember: we rehearsed (for example) Clyde McPhatter and the Drifters' first session for something like six weeks, working every day. . . . At the same time, other legendary indie record men were lining up streetcorner groups in the wings and pushing them out to sing two songs, one take each, and that was the record! They would do four or five groups a night that way. The band didn't even have a chance to learn the chords. And God help us, there is a cult for that shit!"

Jerry is consistently disparaging about vocal group records; he just doesn't respond to the spontaneity, which for many rock fans gives them an engaging charm. "We always went for the long pull," he said. "If a guy couldn't sing, we wouldn't sign him. And there were so many non-singers hitting in the rock 'n' roll period. We had the best roster of singers of any company. We just didn't go for the one-song, one-hit acts."

Jerry's statement is generally true, but Atlantic did occasionally go for a purely pop act. They issued isolated records by white New York singers Paul Evans and Gerry Granahan, and leased independently produced masters by southern rockabilly singers, including Teddy Redell, Bobby Brant, and Sonny West, the composer of Buddy Holly's hits, "Oh, Boy!" and "Rave On." And they tried an intriguing and unique experiment with Tommy Facenda, a former member of Gene Vincent's Bluecaps. They had him record twenty-eight versions of the song "High School, U.S.A.," in which he mentioned by name local high schools in various regions of the country; there was a different record for each of Atlantic's different distributors. The producer of "High School, U.S.A." was Frank Guida, who subsequently did well with his atmospheric productions with Gary "U.S." Bonds. Facenda's record was a sizable national hit, but Atlantic admitted difficulties in ensuring that the right pressing was allocated to its appropriate distributor, and never repeated the concept.

Occasionally, Atlantic chased a record that was selling well on a label too small to be able to handle the problems of national distribution. In 1957 they bid for "Long Lonely Nights," a record that was selling fast in Philadelphia on the local Mainline label, by a previously unknown group called Lee Andrews and the Hearts. But Leonard Chess stepped in with a higher or faster offer and acquired the rights. Dismayed but determined, Ahmet and Jerry rushed Clyde McPhatter into the studio to cover the song and managed to get it out onto the market fast enough to enter the *Billboard* charts the same week. Both records squeezed into the national top 50. Atlantic picked up the rights to a couple of other group records from Mainline, "Lost Love" by the Superiors, and "While Walking" by the Fabulaires, neither of which would be worth mentioning if they were not in exactly that one-take, out-of-key idiom that Atlantic normally abhorred.

"While Walking" was released on Atlantic's East-West subsidiary, a label that issued twenty-five singles during 1957 and 1958 and had only one, minor, hit, "Weekend" by the Kingsmen, who were Bill Haley's Comets. The label was set up to provide an outlet for productions by Lee Hazelwood and his business partner Lester Sill. Lee worked out of Pheonix, Arizona, and Lester was based in Los Angeles; hence the name of the label—Atlantic was "East" and they were "West." But although the Hazelwood-Sill partnership provided a long string of hits for the Philadelphia label, Jamie, by Duane Eddy, they came up with nothing comparable for Atlantic on East-West. Charles Brown recorded a single, but his day seemed to have passed, and the young Oklahoma song writer David Gates had a 45, too, "Walkin' And Talkin'," accompanied by Leon Russell on the piano. More than ten years later, Gates "made it" as writer and singer with Bread, around the same time as Russell emerged as a star in his own right. Their day was a long way off yet.

Atlantic made a much more productive arrangement, also through Lester Sill, with Los Angeles-based song writers Jerry Leiber and Mike Stoller.

V

Jerry Leiber was born and grew up in Baltimore, Maryland. "I was brought up in a mixed neighborhood, and there were a lot of Negro workers in the area who came up from the South to work in the plants during the war, and I'd imagine that just the proximity of living near them had a great effect on my life. I moved to California when I was twelve and started writing lyrics when I was sixteen or seventeen." Which was about the time when Mike Stoller first met him. Mike had been at Los Angeles City College for about a term, and was a year or two older.

"I got a call from Jerry, who I'd never met, who said he'd got my name from a friend of his, and had heard I could write notes—music—on paper. I said, 'So what?' He said, 'Well I'm writing songs.' He was very matter-of-fact, business-like. I said, 'Well I don't really like songs —which was true—and I also threw in a couple of pretentious references to Stravinsky.

"But he was persistent, said he'd like to meet me. So I agreed to meet him, although I wasn't enthusiastic about it. Anyway he came to the house and I opened the door and I just looked at him for a while—he had fiery red hair, and one blue eye and one brown eye. So after about three months of just standing there I said come on in. He showed me the lyrics he'd written, in his school book—we were both seventeen at the time. I could see from the ditto lines under the first lines of most verses that a lot of them were blues. He said yes.

"I liked the blues too; I had always liked the blues. It was somehow a lot closer to reality than a lot of popular culture, especially movies and songs. When Jerry had said song writing, I had thought he meant something else. Whenever I could, I used to play a kind of blues piano, 'cause I had liked boogie woogie piano since I was a kid.

Leiber and Stoller. The first team of freelance song-writers to establish a separate royalty as independent producers. Their productions for Atlantic of the Coasters and the Drifters brought new standards of wit, musicianship, and discipline which affected the sound and style of all subsequent popular music. Above: Outside of the West Coast office of Atlantic Records, Melrose Avenue, Los Angeles, in 1956. Clockwise: Jerry Leiber, Lester Sill, Mike Stoller, and Lou Krefetz, then Atlantic's sales manager. At right: Leiber and Stoller at work, 1959.

My idols were Pinetop Smith, Albert Ammons, Meade Lux Lewis.

"Jerry worked at a record store on Fairfax Avenue right near Fairfax High School, and while he was there he met Lester Sill, who worked as a promotion man for Modern Records, and who had a big thing for the blues."

Until Capitol was formed in Hollywood in 1942, there had been few companies based on the West Coast, but by 1948 when Mike and Jerry came together, a very active scene had developed, especially in the rhythm and blues field. Exclusive, Aladdin, Imperial, Modern, and Specialty were the best known among as many as 100 independent companies based in Los Angeles and the San Francisco-Oakland Bay area. Apart from the enterprising men who founded and managed these companies, there were other important figures working on the sidelines, among whom Lester Sill was especially famous. Over a period of twenty-five years he had provided moral and economic support for many talented writers and producers, helping to launch the careers of Phil Spector, Lou Adler, Carole King, and David Gates; but perhaps his most important contribution was his encouragement to Leiber and Stoller during their early years in the business. According to Mike:

"At one time Lester used to go down to Dolphins of Hollywood—which wasn't in Hollywood at all, it was at Central and One hundred and sixty-fourth in the ghetto area of Los Angeles—and he used to go in there with his records and he would have a pocket full of sand, and he would put a seventy-eight on the machine and put the sand on the floor and do a shuffle dance to show how good the record was.

"So Lester heard Jerry singing in the store and got talking to him, found out he wrote songs and then that he and I were working together and he set up an appointment for us at Modern Records. We went along to meet one of the Biharis, and after we had waited about twenty minutes past the time of our appointment we got very upset and walked out. Just down the street was Aladdin Records, so we went in there and they bought two of our songs.

"Then Gene Norman, a disc jockey who put on a blues jamboree every year, gave us the names and addresses of all the people who were going to be on his show that year, and we called them up and went round visiting all of them—Wynonie Harris, Helen Humes—all around Central Avenue and West Adams—Charles Brown, Amos Milburn, Floyd Dixon, Jimmy Witherspoon—and we set up the show for Gene, and Witherspoon took one of our songs, and later recorded it. All of this was very exciting for us.

"We went back to the Mesners at Aladdin, and they took another song which we rehearsed with Charles Brown—"Hard Times"—which was our first chart record. This was at the time when there were regional R and B charts, and our record made some of those."

Still working sporadically, Leiber and Stoller began to get more regular commissions after 1951, when the Cincinnati label King formed the Federal subsidiary, with Ralph Bass as A and R man.

"Ralph would call us and say he had a session fixed up for a singer but didn't have material, could we get to the studio with four songs, and sometimes we'd get there with less than four and have to sit down and write one while the others were being recorded. And since there were no lead sheets, we had to teach them how to sing the songs and in effect did the production job although of course we weren't being paid in that capacity. But we were happy just to be doing the work."

Through this period, the record business had a casual attitude to legal definitions of contracts and royalties.

"Sometimes we would be given a mimeographed scrap of paper that was meant to be a contract, other times we got documents that were very legitimate-looking. Some of these companies had a policy of mistreating their artists who wrote material, I guess on the basis that many of the artists weren't too literate, and it was easy to please them by buying fancy cars, and I guess because we wrote for these singers we were treated the same way, and we were exploited a great deal at the time. We didn't see any other people like us who wrote songs. There were a few A and R men who got their names on records as writers, but we never knew if they wrote them. We were the youngest ofays writing blues that we knew of."

Two of the standards that Leiber and Stoller wrote in the period were "K. C. Lovin' " (in 1952) later retitled "Kansas City," and "Hound Dog" (in 1953). Both songs have been claimed by and ascribed to other song writers, but Mike described matter-of-factly how they came into existence.

"We rehearsed 'K. C. Lovin' with Little Willie Littlefield at Maxwell Davis' house—Maxwell was to be the arranger for the session, which was for Federal. The jumpy little bass figure was in that when I played the song to Little Willie."

"Hound Dog" has a more complicated history. When it was originally issued in a version by Willie Mae Thornton on Peacock in 1953, the song was credited to Johnny Otis, but when it was recorded again by Elvis Presley for RCA in 1956, it was ascribed to Leiber and Stoller. Johnny Otis was a West Coast bandleader who had a knack of finding good musicians and singers, and a flair for presenting them in an entertaining package show. He "discovered" Willie Mae Thornton at an audition in Houston, and recognized "Hound Dog" as being ideal material for her. According

to Johnny, the three of them—Leiber, Stoller, and he—
wrote it together.

"I met Leiber and Stoller at a record distributor in Los
Angeles. They were young kids, and they said we write
songs, maybe we can do some things together, and I said
okay. And they would bring songs, and I would help rewrite
them. For instance, once they had a song that had razor-
cuttin' and gin-drinkin' and dice-shootin', and they didn't
understand, this was derogatory to black people. They were
just young guys who meant well, they weren't racist in
the true sense of the word.

"We did a lot of songs together—'The Candle's Burnin'
Low,' 'Main Liner,' and of course 'Hound Dog.' When
that came out, owing to an error by Don Robey [Duke
and Peacock Records], the label had my name on but
didn't have Leiber and Stoller's name on, although it
should have. But we straightened that out between us.
Then when Elvis Presley did his version, they cut me out,
by some legal maneuver called 'disaffirm the contract,'
which they could do because they'd been under twenty-one
when we wrote 'Hound Dog.'"

Mike Stoller has a different story to tell. "Jerry and I
had written 'Hound Dog,' and Johnny Otis, who was a
bandleader and entrepreneur, saw it and said he thought
he knew who might record it, and in return for getting
it recorded he would take a third of the publishing rights.
The next thing we knew, Willie Mae Thornton's version
was out, as we'd written it, but with Johnny's name on
it."

Leiber and Stoller went to court to set things straight
with Don Robey and made sure that regardless of whose
name was credited as author on the label, they got the
money. When Elvis Presley cut his version, things got
more complicated. Presley's manager Tom Parker liked

his boy to record songs that his publishing company owned. Ideally, song writers agreed to give Elvis half the songwriting credit too, but in the case of "Hound Dog," matters were already complicated enough; the simplest thing would be to buy up the publishing rights. So Hill and Range Songs, on behalf of Elvis Presley Music, bought half the publishing rights from Robey's publishing firm, Lion Music. Even that had its repercussions, though; Johnny Otis had been signed to a third publishing company, Valjo (a subsidiary of King Records), at the time "Hound Dog" had been written, and in October 1956 Valjo took out a suit against Elvis Presley Music—and Jerry Leiber and Mike Stoller—which accused them of conspiring to deprive Valjo of the publishing rights to "Hound Dog," which had by then sold over two million copies.

It all went to show, you couldn't be too careful who you did business with. Leiber and Stoller took steps to protect themselves. Mike describes their experience with their own label: they set up Spark Records in Los Angeles.

"After our experience with 'Hound Dog,' where because of our age and inexperience we really got screwed around, we got the idea of starting a record company and publishing company of our own, so we wouldn't have this problem of collecting royalties that were due to us. Some of the companies had special deals whereby the song writers were getting a half a cent per record sold, instead of two cents.

"So my dad and a friend of Lester Sill put up about thirty-five thousand dollars each and we started a record company, publishing company, and distributing company. In the office we had an old school desk back-to-back with an old sofa; two steps in front of that was a piano, and behind that was a filing cabinet. There was also a john, and that was it.

"We started rehearsing the Robins, a vocal group that had started out with the Johnny Otis Show, but had since left, and in the meantime recorded a couple of acts in San Francisco, a group and Linda Hopkins. We sold the master of Linda's session to Crystalette Records. And we brought a duo called Willie and Ruth down, and did the original recording of 'Love Me,' which I think Jerry would agree was the worst song we ever did."

Jerry Leiber's idols were Lorenz Hart, Cole Porter, Irving Berlin: "I admired them and tried very hard to write like them. But I couldn't, it never came out that way." Instead, it came out like the Cheers' "Black Denim Trousers And Motorcycle Boots," Leiber and Stoller's first pop hit, which they produced for Capitol. But although the story line was good, the arrangement and vocal harmonies were in the current pop idiom, so the Cheers' record doesn't hold up today, especially compared to a masterpiece Leiber and Stoller had produced some months before on their own Spark label—"Riot In Cell Block Number Nine," by the Robins. The lead singer takes the role of a rebellious prisoner; he describes a tense prison insurrection which is finally brought under control by guards; but menacing implications linger. Actually, the lead singer was not a member of the Robins. Apparently nobody in the group could provide the necessary tone to carry the message, so West Coast singer-song writer Richard Berry was used anonymously for the first-person lead; his interpretation did justice to the near-protest lyric which fades at the end with drums hammering a warning of what might happen in the future. Four years later, Leiber and Stoller couldn't reproduce the authenticity of "Cell Block Number Nine" when they wrote "Jailhouse Rock" for Elvis Presley. "Not surprisingly," observed Jerry, "since in the film we had to deal with the contradiction of having a fifty-piece orchestra playing offstage. It's harder to capture a prison atmosphere in those conditions. I think we used just four instruments on the Robins' record."

Each of the Robins' several Spark singles was selling quite well on the West Coast, around 90,000 copies, if Mike remembers right, but they weren't selling at all anywhere else. Nesuhi Ertegun, who was on the West Coast at the time, took an interest in the song-writing partnership, and put them in touch with Atlantic in New York. Jerry Leiber and Lester Sill went to New York and set up a deal where Atlantic bought up all the Spark masters and contracted Leiber and Stoller to keep working as producers with the Robins. The song writers could still work for other labels, including RCA, which according to Mike was a pioneering step in the restructuring of the record business: "I think that was the first independent production contract ever made."

The first issue on Atco under the new arrangement was a re-release of "Smokey Joe's Cafe," and with national distribution it sold 250,000. But the Robins' managers balked at what was happening, and held onto the group's name and two of the singers. Leiber and Stoller brought in two replacements and renamed the group the Coasters, whom they continued to record on the West Coast until 1957. The group's really big pop hit, "Young Blood"/"Searchin'," was cut in L.A. It came out in February 1957 and was still on the charts in October; first "Young Blood" was the hit and then it got turned over and "Searchin" got played.

That record confirmed that the song-writing pair had a magic touch, and for the three years that followed, they almost never failed to have at least one song on the charts, usually by either Elvis Presley or the Coasters, sometimes by both at the same time.

Leiber and Stoller got involved with Presley almost by accident. Mike recalls, "We didn't know that Presley was going to do 'Hound Dog.' I'd heard his previous record, 'Heartbreak Hotel,' [written by a Florida school teacher,

Mae Axton], but then I went to Europe with the first sizable royalty check I saw [from "Smokey Joe's Cafe"], and when I came back Jerry met me off the boat and said Presley did 'Hound Dog,' and I said good, but I didn't know what it meant. A few days later, it was number one."

By a fortunate coincidence, Leiber and Stoller had assigned their publishing company to the same New York publishing house—Hill and Range—that handled Elvis Presley's publishing company. So while song writers with other publishing companies had difficulty in getting Elvis to hear their songs, Leiber and Stoller could reach him through the Aberbach brothers who owned Hill and Range. Mike explained, "We suggested to the Aberbachs at Hill and Range that Elvis might do 'Love Me,' which I felt might have a commercial appeal—actually we threw quite a few at them, and Elvis chose that one. It was never issued as a single, but the Extended Play record that it was on made the charts. And after the success of that, following 'Hound Dog,' and because of our association with Gene and Julian Aberbach at Hill and Range, who were both our publishers and Elvis' publishers, we were able to work quite often with him."

Leiber and Stoller did most of the songs for Elvis' films *Loving You* and *Jailhouse Rock,* and for a short time held a job at the RCA-Victor office in New York. "It was meant to be a year's job but it lasted two months because none of the five records we made for them was a hit, whereas the one we did with Atlantic during that time was a smash." Not only did Atlantic records seem to sell better, Mike remembered them being more fun to make.

"When we first moved to New York, we would travel from Hill and Range's office to Atlantic's, our office was in our briefcase. We would walk into Atlantic almost every day, use their conference room for an office, barge in on Ahmet and Jerry, who had their office in one room, or on Herb Abramson, who had his down the hall. And we'd stay until one of them asked us politely if we'd leave, they had something private to talk about.

"With most of the other independents, we had the feeling that if any record did well, we would get screwed somehow. But with Atlantic we thought we'd get paid. The experience of working at RCA, my memory of it was that it was like walking into an insurance office, and immediately all creativity, all inspiration was drained. It was depressing, I couldn't work under those circumstances."

Leiber and Stoller's most valuable contributions to Atlantic records were records by the Coasters from 1957 to 1961, and by the Drifters from 1959 to 1963. The Coasters' "Young Blood"/"Searchin' " became Atlantic's first top 10 hit during the summer of 1957, while "Yakety Yak" by the same group was the company's first national number 1 almost exactly a year later. Between the two hits came several Coasters records that failed to register, including "Idol With The Golden Head," a minor hit, and "Sweet Georgia Brown" and "Gee Golly" which didn't make the Hot 100 at all. It wasn't easy getting public response to the Coasters' style. The problem was to make the meticulously contrived records sound spontaneous. According to Jerry Leiber:

"We spent many hours in the studios with the Coasters, overdubbing their performances because with their material it was critical that the timing, the jokes fall right. Which is another type of recording really, it's a lot more plastic, a lot more clinical than going for a great soul performance on a Ray Charles record, or those records with Joe Turner or Ruth Brown, which were usually third or fourth or fifth take: there were no twenty-six takes, or thirty-one takes, or six hours of overdubbing two bars of music, like we did with the Coasters."

Mike Stoller remembers hours spent perfecting Coasters' records. "We would do things like cutting esses off

Best Wishes,
The Coasters

The Coasters, cool clowns who breathed life into Leiber and Stoller pictures.

words, sticking the tape back together so you didn't notice. And sometimes if the first refrain on a take was good and the second one lousy, we'd tape another recording of the first one and stick it in the place of the second one. Before multitrack recording, this was."

But Leiber and Stoller became more adept at their techniques, disc jockeys and record buyers grew accustomed to their style of humor, and the hits came more consistently. After "Yakety Yak," "The Shadow Knows" missed the charts, but then in succession "Charlie Brown,"

"Along Came Jones," "Poison Ivy"/"I'm A Hog For You Baby," "What About Us," "Besame Mucho," "Wake Me, Shake Me," "Shoppin' For Clothes," "Wait A Minute," and "Little Egypt" were all hits. One interesting quality of the Coasters records was the sparseness of the accompaniment, in an era when pop productions were becoming increasingly elaborate as advances in recording techniques allowed more instruments to be recorded with clarity. Atlantic's engineer Tom Dowd was very impressed with their self-restraint:

"Leiber and Stoller made no fuss about the idea of the multitrack machine. When we first got it, during the post mortems after a session I'd play them acetates to compare takes, and they'd say oh, can you do that? when I had added something to a track. And next time they started saying omit that, leave this out, we can put it in later if we need it. And they didn't commit that crime of piling everything in at the session and then trying to pull it out later when they listened to the tracks, which was how a lot of other producers reacted to the introduction of multi-track facilities.

"They got it down so that they were making their Coasters' records with four pieces—Mike on piano; and a drum, a bass, and a guitar. And perhaps King Curtis on saxophone. And that was all. They didn't go for four guitars, three extra percussion, and 'We'll take them out if they don't fit.'"

Of course the Coasters' records weren't purely Leiber and Stoller. The singers in the group were unusually adaptable. As Jerry Leiber points out, "Billy Guy had a marvelous sense of timing, and the dirtiest, the most lascivious voice." It's Billy's voice that gives the conviction to "Searchin'," "Little Egypt," and "Shoppin' For Clothes." The last of these was written by Kent Harris, one of the few Coasters records of this period not written by Leiber

King Curtis, one of the most versatile accompanists in popular music, who stuttered anxiously on "Yakety Yak," sighed sympathetically on "Shoppin' For Clothes," and ten years later found exactly the right sound to fit into Aretha Franklin's "Bridge Over Troubled Water": pure, ethereal.

and Stoller. A remarkable cameo from city life, it portrayed the singer as a customer in a department store, trying to buy a suit on credit, and failing; King Curtis, whose distinctive stuttering sax was a feature of the faster Coasters' records like "Yakety Yak" and "Charlie Brown," was here subdued and gently sympathetic. Four years earlier, a West Coast singer called Boogaloo had recorded the song as a monologue called "Clothes Line," but his version was cluttered with too many words and a clumsy chorus refrain. Leiber and Stoller's interpretation through the Coasters confirmed their genius for producing situation comedy songs, in the way they pared down the lyric and simplified the arrangement. "Shoppin' For Clothes" wasn't much of a hit, but Jerry Leiber remembers that it was always a "house favorite."

The records that Leiber and Stoller made with the Drifters had an entirely different character from those with the Coasters. First, they used a much denser accompaniment, often including orchestral backup. "There Goes My Baby," the first Drifters' record by the renamed Five Crowns featuring Benny King as lead singer, is even given credit—or blame—for introducing strings into rhythm and blues records. Actually, the Skyliners' "Since I Don't Have You" had been a hit of a couple of months earlier in 1959, and it featured a full string section, with a pizzicato "break." Still, "There Goes My Baby" certainly used strings in an unconventional way, more like a sax section might have been used.

But for Mike Stoller, the more important innovation in the Drifters' records was the rhythm. "Jerry and I both liked the baion, a Brazilian rhythm that has this beat." He taps out the dramatic bullfighting beats. "After it worked in 'There Goes My Baby,' we used it a lot. I would almost say to death, but other people used it too.

"The rhythm should have been played by a tympani

Above: the two most famous lead singers from the Drifters, although each of them was with the group for less than two years: Clyde McPhatter (left) in 1953–54, and Ben E. King (right), in 1959–60. Below: the most prolific Drifters lineup, with Johnny Moore (second from right) as lead. Produced by Bert Berns, Jerry Wexler, and others, this lineup had a number of American hits in the mid-sixties, some of which belatedly became hits in Britain in 1971–72.

player, but there wasn't one, so the drummer played, and he didn't change the pitch at all, which has interesting consequences. It was the first rhythm and blues record I know of that had strings on it—it had a sound that we could hear in the arrangement, a pretentious Rimski-Korsakov-Borodin pseudo line."

Through all the Brazilian rhythm and Russian backup Benny King wailed in a high, gospel-inflected style. In contrast to Leiber and Stoller's tongue-in-cheek love songs for the Coasters (e.g. "I'm a hog for you baby and I can't get enough of your love"), "There Goes My Baby" was a simple declaration of eternal love written by an ex-member of the Five Crowns, with lines of uneven length like an abstract nonrhyming poem. "The studio was pretty bad too," Mike remembers; "the sound was swimming around. Jerry Wexler told us to go and do it again, but we said no, let's try to do something with what we got, and Tommy Dowd worked on it, cleaned it up. Even so, whenever I heard it on the radio, I kept thinking I was getting two different stations on the same wavelength."

Unwilling or unable to supply suitably innocent love songs for the Drifters, Leiber and Stoller commissioned songs from several teams of song writers, and unwittingly generated a "school" of New York writers which dominated American pop music from 1960 until 1964, when the Beatles brought the idea of the organic song writing, singing, and instrument-playing unit to the American record business. For the second time, Atlantic had paved the way for other record companies by structuring the process in which a particular idiom was recorded. Just as Jesse Stone's "rock 'n' roll arrangements" had earlier provided imitators with a pattern to follow, Leiber and Stoller's concept of recording vocal groups was imitated and developed by several producers, the more successful of whom included Luther Dixon with the Shirelles, Phil Spector with the Crystals and the Ronettes, various Motown producers with the Miracles, Temptations, and others, and Bert Berns, who took on the job of producing the Drifters for Atlantic when Leiber and Stoller had had enough.

Apart from the Detroit-based Motown producers, who used local writers, all of these producers used material written by New York writers, many of whom were affiliated with the same publishing company, Aldon, which was managed by Don Kirshner. But the first writers to supply hit songs for the Drifters were Jerome "Doc" Pomus and Mort Shuman, who were affiliated with Leiber and Stoller's publishers, Aberbach. Pomus and Shuman had already written one national hit before they started working with the Drifters, a classic expression of adolescent anguish called "Teenager In Love," which the white New York group Dion and the Belmonts sang with a simple rhythm accompaniment. Their first two hits with the Drifters, "True Love, True Love" and "This Magic Moment" used dramatic, elaborate arrangements in the style of "There Goes My Baby," but the third, "Save The Last Dance For Me," was smoother, with less obvious gospel and Russian influences. The Brazilian baion rhythm still identified a "Drifters" sound, but Benny King's voice was in a lower register and the string section played a more conventional background harmony. "Save The Last Dance" had another classic teen lyric, with the singer big-heartedly granting his girl license to roam the dance floor provided she remembered to return to him at the end. It was the first Drifters' record to top the national pop charts, and provided model and inspiration for all the New York vocal group records that followed, most of which were written in a hothouse in the Brill building under Don Kirshner's supervision.

The Brill building is at 1619 Broadway, and has been the "home" of independent New York publishing com-

The Dimension label, a spin-off from Atlantic's Leiber and Stoller productions, had as its first record a smash called "The Loco-Motion," and here's the picture to prove it. After furnishing hits for the Drifters and others, publishers Don Kirshner and Don Nevins (left) launched Dimension, featuring songs by their own writers, including Gerry Goffin and Carole King (right). Little Eva was the singer on "The Loco-Motion" (front).

panies since 1945. Almost every glass-paneled door has a different name stenciled on it, and each publisher is hoping to get his songs recorded by a potential hit singer. In the late fifties, Don Kirshner seemed to draw to him an unusually big proportion of exceptional writers, perhaps partly because he had direct access to some successful singers, notably Bobby Darin and Connie Francis, who were both consistently in the charts from 1958 through 1963. Among the writers attached to Kirshner's Aldon Music in this period were Neil Sedaka, Howard Greenfield, and Jack Keller (these three combined had supplied several hits for Connie Francis), Gerry Goffin and Carole King, and Barry Mann and Cynthia Weil.

The procedure for a publisher at this time was to make a rough demonstration record of a new song, which was then submitted to producers for their consideration. Kirshner introduced a new concept, by making demos of very high quality, sometimes employing a full orchestra, so that a producer simply had to copy every detail of the demo when making his commercial recording. As Kirshner also made a point of using good singers on his demonstration records, it soon became apparent that his demos were good enough to release as they were, and after leasing a couple of national hits to Epic by his demo singer Tony Orlando, Kirshner formed his own label, Dimension, which had hits by the Cookies, Little Eva, and song writer Carole King. All of which might have happened even if Leiber and Stoller had never used a song from Kirshner, but as Tony Orlando recalls events, the work with the Drifters was an essential step in the development of both the individual writers at Aldon and the company as a whole, to say nothing of Tony's own career.

According to Tony, the sound and effect of Pomus and Shuman's "Save The Last Dance For Me" had a profound influence on Gerry Goffin and Carole King, who had by then (fall of 1960) written a number of songs that had been recorded but didn't sell. Tony was the singer at a session which produced demos for four songs which were submitted as possible follow-ups to "Save The Last Dance."

"We did 'Will You Still Love Me Tomorrow,' 'Some Kind Of Wonderful,' 'Halfway To Paradise,' and 'Bless You.' Eventually, the first became a big hit for the Shirelles, the second *was* a hit for the Drifters, and the other two were issued as we recorded them, under my name, on Epic. If you listen to those records, you can hear how Gerry and Carole were preoccupied with that 'Drifters' sound. Although melodically 'Will You Still Love Me Tomorrow' is very different from 'Save The Last Dance For Me,' chordwise they're very similar, and in her head Carole thought she had written a song like Pomus and Shuman would have done it. And all through the session, Gerry Goffin kept telling me to do this Benny King hum, he wanted me to fill every space between the lines with a hum like Benny had." Having gained confidence by using the Pomus-Shuman style as a model, Goffin and King became one of the most prolific and successful song-writing teams of the era, supplying more songs for the Shirelles (on the recently formed New York label, Scepter) and Bobby Vee (on Liberty), among many.

From 1960 through 1964, the Drifters were Atlantic's most consistent hit-makers, espcially after Bobby Darin was lured to Capitol in 1962. The main reason for the group's endurance was their outstanding song material. Refusing to abandon all standards and simply record whatever teen ballads came into the office, Leiber and Stoller, and later Bert Berns, rigorously sifted out songs which presented strong situations and had good melodic and harmonic constructions. From Goffin and King they took the outstanding "Up On The Roof," and from Barry Mann and Cynthia Weil "I'll Take You Home" and "On Broadway." Burt Bacharach and Hal David, who later became celebrated for their work with Dionne Warwick, wrote their first songs together for the Drifters, "Please Stay" and "Mexican Divorce," and incidentally discovered Dionne Warwick at a Drifters session where she was one of the backup singers.

Leiber and Stoller were able to turn one apparent setback to advantage when Benny King decided to leave the Drifters to try to make it as a solo act. A singer with a similar voice, Rudy Lewis, was drafted into the group as a replacement, while Leiber and Stoller took on Benny as a separate assignment. One of Benny's first singles was yet another song of urban teen love with a baion rhythm, "Spanish Harlem," written by Jerry Leiber in conjunction with Phil Spector.

As a teenager in Los Angeles, Spector produced a national number 1 in 1958 with his first record, "To Know Him Is To Love Him" by the Teddy Bears, but had been unable to follow through. Three years later he decided to go to New York, and Lester Sill told him to look up Leiber and Stoller when he got there. Mike Stoller remembered being impressed with Spector's ideas in the studio. "We signed him up to write and produce for us, gave him some advances, and Jerry Leiber let him stay at his home for a while. Phil started writing, with Jerry and some other people, and Jerry took him to a lot of sessions, employed him on quite a few as guitarist. We got him a job producing at Big Top Records, and he did Ray Peterson's 'Corrine Corrine,' that was late 1960. And then he made a separate deal with Atlantic, breaking our contract by saying he signed it when he was under twenty-one. Which wasn't a nice thing to do.

"But Phil really wasn't very successful with Atlantic, who were into a heavier blues-oriented sound than he was, and he went off to form his own label, Philles, with Lester Sill. And had all those hits with the Crystals, the Ronettes, Righteous Brothers."

Even after his own Philles records started to do well,

Spector continued to play on occasional Drifters records. He played the celebrated blues guitar break that emerges out of the strings in "On Broadway," the last big hit that Leiber and Stoller produced with the Drifters, in 1963. In 1964, perhaps impressed with Spector's success on his own, Leiber and Stoller formed the Red Bird label, in co-partnership with George Goldner, who had sold all his interests in Roulette to Morris Levy. For two years, Red Bird had extraordinary success with the girl group sound that had evolved as an "answer" to the Drifters' records. The Dixie Cups, the Jelly Beans, and the Shangri Las all made the national top 10. But by 1966, Leiber and Stoller had had enough. Although their company was hugely successful, they had been reduced to being administrators. Many of the songs were written by Jeff Barry and Ellie Greenwich, sometimes in association with Spector, and much of the production was done by the engineer George "Shadow" Morton. Leiber and Stoller sold their interest in Red Bird, and retired from the scene to write a Broadway musical.

By coincidence, that was the year that the Drifters disappeared from the pop charts too, after two years with Bert Berns, whom Jerry Wexler brought in to produce the group when Leiber and Stoller phased themselves out in 1964. Berns composed several famous pop songs which used a standard Latin American chord sequence, including "Twist And Shout," "Piece Of My Heart," and "Hang On Sloopy," and as a fan of Latin music was easily able to sustain the baion rhythms that were associated with Drifters recordings. "Under The Boardwalk," which was recorded at one of his first sessions with the group, took the Drifters back into the national top 10 in 1964, but for the last time. The attractive singing, infectious melody, and evocative lyric of "Under The Boardwalk" enabled this record to compete with the current onslaught of British records, but its follow-ups were apparently too clearly contrived for the times. Only Motown productions, with more attacking rhythms, intense singing, and gospel harmonies, could match the sales of the British groups who played their own instruments. But as his records with the Drifters declined in sales, Bert Berns had the strange experience of hearing a cover of "Twist And Shout" by the Beatles on the radio. The same year, 1964, Herman's Hermits had their first hit with the Goffin and King song, "I'm Into Something Good" and the Searchers disinterred Leiber and Stoller's "Love Potion Number Nine." Bert jumped in and swam with the tide. Backed by the three heads of Atlantic, he formed Bang! Records (B-ert, A-hmet, N-esuhi, G-erald) and in 1965 had hits with the McCoys while also producing Them and Lulu in London, for British Decca.

Atlantic's chiefs meanwhile sold their publishing company, Progressive, to provide themselves with some personal capital, although the company continued to improve on profits each year except 1964. They survived by leasing masters, contracting independent producers, and acting as distributor for independent labels. That the company survived at all was due to the unusual determination and resourcefulness of its senior executives, for it was in this same period that most of the other survivors of the indie era fell by the wayside, or severely curtailed their activity in the business. Archie Bleyer of Cadence retired from the record business while he was still winning, after his major artists (Andy Williams, the Everly Brothers) had moved to other labels, without spending a lot of money trying to repeat their successes with less talented performers. Leonard Chess kept his Chess label going with some success, and Morris Levy of Roulette was the first East Coast record man to discover the nostalgic value of a catalogue not yet ten years old by repackaging recent hits as "Golden Goodies." But during the early sixties, Lew Chudd sold Imperial to Liberty, Hy Weiss passed Old Town to MGM, and Sam Phillips reduced his Sun output to a trickle, as Art Rupe had already done with Specialty. Gradually but perceptibly, Ahmet Ertegun and Jerry Wexler began to emerge as resourceful veterans of the record business.

To survive, a record man needed not only to know what a hit record sounded like, and how to get it made: he also had to get it played.

EIGHT:
SOUTHERN RED NECKS
AND
THE NEW YORK JEW

Atlantic Records managed to survive and grow through the 1960s because Ahmet and Jerry were flexible enough to abandon most of the canons upon which they had based their actions during the 1950s. By the end of the sixties, a major record company stood in the place of the struggling and insecure independent of a few years before.

Viewed from today, the development seems to have a logic, as if Ahmet and Jerry, conscious of their own goal, had deliberately taken a series of decisions to make their company big, rich, and powerful. But back in 1962 the view over Jerry's shoulder into the future was uncertain and largely unimaginable.

During the fifties, Atlantic pioneered techniques for the arranging of forms of music which had previously been spontaneous, contriving first a New York rock 'n' roll style out of an imitation of southern dance blues, and then an organized vocal group sound where there had been nothing but doo-wahs. This approach to popular music, of identifying the elements of a style and putting them together with care and purpose, dominated until 1964, when a huge reaction became clearly visible.

The reaction against arranged pop music was not absolute: in Detroit, teams of producers under Berry Gordy carried synthetic spontaneity to new levels of contrivance and success, with a spectacular series of hits from Marvin Gaye, the Miracles, the Temptations, the Supremes, and many others. But while the Tamla, Gordy, and Motown labels thrived on an extension of previous techniques, elsewhere the old approach yielded to new ones. The new techniques developed in two principal areas, Britain and the American South.

In Britain the distinctive characteristic of the new music was a group that played its own accompaniment, and often wrote its own material. In the South, the arranger's role was diminished by units of session men who, instead of playing written arrangements which represented a producer's concept, evolved their own "head arrangements," jam session "grooves" which were gradually rationalized to accommodate verse structures of songs. Atlantic's growth during the 1960s resulted from the company's productive alliance with both centers: Ahmet and Nesuhi made arrangements that brought British acts to Atlantic, and Jerry made contacts in the South.

Like most innovations, the Southern Groove had been around for a few years before it was widely recognized and categorized. Although early examples of the sound can be identified retrospectively on records made in 1959 in New Orleans (notably "Ooh Poo Pah Doo" by Jesse Hill on Minit) and Memphis ("Smokie" by the Bill Black Combo on Hi), Atlantic was not involved at all until 1961, and

Jerry Wexler and Veronica ("Ronnie") Bennett dance the Mashed Potato. Veronica later became lead singer of the Ronettes and then Mrs. Phil Spector.

not intimately until 1964. Up to 1964, Atlantic producers in New York were still doing things the old way, clever producers and arrangers closely supervising every musician, possibly allowing a guitarist or a saxophone player the freedom to improvise an obligato harmony or a break at the bridge, but still minimizing the effectiveness of what he did by smothering the overall sound in swirling strings and cooing vocal choruses.

Leiber and Stoller continued to provide the bulk of Atlantic's hits through the Drifters, the Coasters, and Ben E. King. Ahmet and Jerry, now working separately, made occasional trips to the studios, but were basically administrators. Ahmet never did set much store by office work, but Jerry was overseer to the staff, hiring and firing, supervising the promotion team of Norm Rubin and Larry Maxwell. Rubin, who has since left Atlantic to become a very effective promoter for United Artists Music, still functions according to the canon he picked up from working under Jerry. Says Rubin: "Jerry used to say, 'Always return a phone call, because you never know who's who. A guy may be nobody today, but a somebody tomorrow. And a guy who's somebody today might be a nobody tomorrow, because he didn't return a phone call.' "

Rubin pulls out his wallet and carefully unfolds a telegram, saved since his wedding day in 1964: DEEPEST REGRETS UNABLE TO ATTEND YOUR WEDDING SINCEREST WISHES FOR FUTURE HAPPINESS GOD SPEED YOUR TRIP TO CALIFORNIA AND DONT FORGET SOLOMON BURKE RELEASE. J. W.

This confusion of domestic and public affairs is still entirely typical of Jerry's life style. He doesn't seem to feel any distinction between family life and business life, which earns him the admiration of other people in the record business, if it does not always endear him to his family. Even now, when he has apparently escaped from the hurly burly of New York to spend winters in his Florida outpost, he is still tracked down by all kinds of people in the music business, most of whom have none of Jerry's interest in books, movies, or modern painting. Jerry's bookcases aren't false fronts to cabinets of booze, but shelves holding obscure modern novels that he has somehow found time to read. But if he would prefer a quiet hour or two with a recent southern novel he has just discovered, he gives no sign of impatience as he gets up to open the door to the latest in an apparently endless stream of visitors, and he keeps an attentive face toward whoever it is—an Atlantic artist recording at the nearby Criteria studios, an out-of-work disc jockey, an R and B fan, a retired promotion man—and breaks off only to answer the phone. You never know who it might be.

One of these visitors drew from Jerry the story of how he returned to active producing, and how Atlantic made its contact with the Southern Groove: Joe Galkin, once a mainstay in Atlantic's southern promotion team, now retired and apparently doing his best to emulate Jerry's life style, with a house and a yacht in Florida. Since Joe and Jerry more or less staged a reminiscence especially for my cassette, it's best to report it as a dialogue. Jerry began: "It was some time in 1961, and I'd been stale in the studio. Clyde was gone, Ray Charles was gone, Ahmet was working with Bobby Darin, Leiber and Stoller had things tied up for us with the Coasters and the Drifters. And I was just administrating in the office, chasing up debts, negotiating with managers, hiring staff when we needed somebody. And Paul Ackerman at *Billboard* used to tell me, 'Get Solomon Burke, you must sign Solomon, he's great.' But Solomon was contracted to Apollo, and I'd say, 'Yeah, Paul, I will, when he's free.'

"So one day my secretary Norene says to me, 'Solomon Burke is waiting outside to see you. I go outside and I

Above: Jerry Wexler in the studio with Solomon Burke. At right: Bert Berns, Atlantic's favorite son from 1964 to 1965.

say, 'Come on in, Solomon, we'll write out the contract.' He said, 'What are you talkin' about?' and I said, 'Stop talkin' will ya, you're on Atlantic.'

"Well around that time Paul had sent me a country and western record, on Four Star, called 'Just Out Of Reach,' suggesting it would be a good record for a black singer to cut. So Paul Ackerman was responsible for our getting both Solomon Burke and the song that made him. I did it with Ray Ellis arranging, flexible head-type things. We cut three or four sides, and first we put out something else, not 'Just Out Of Reach,' I think it was a song called 'How Many Times.' It bombed. Then we put out 'Just Out Of Reach' and nothing happened with it until Joe called us and said he'd got some stations playing it in the South."

JOE: Yeah, this is how I got with Atlantic. I called Jerry up one day and said to him, "Jerry, I'm calling from a station in Charlotte, North Carolina. I know you've got two good promotion men down here, but you've got a song I think I can work with, it's called 'Just Out Of Reach' by Solomon Burke."

JERRY: I told him, you gotta be crazy, but I'm getting excited because I'd really hoped that something might happen with it.

JOE: But he tells me I'm wasting my time, what about the Coasters and the Drifters? And I say, you don't need me for those records, I like working with the little ones that nobody's heard of. So he says, okay, well what do you want, and I made a deal with him for three weeks.

JERRY: You can tell him how much I gave you.

JOE: He gave me fifty dollars a week.

JERRY: He was askin' me for a hundred, and I said, you're crazy. . . .

JOE: Yeah, he said, "You're crazy, the bum ain't worth that much." So, I took it, and we got pick hits on a couple of stations. The first week, we sold three hundred records. I called Jerry, told him I thought we had a smash. The second week was about one thousand, the third was two thousand. I called Jerry and said we got a hit, and he said no you haven't, get down to New Orleans, and a few other places, just send me the bill. I even got some country stations playing it.

JERRY: By the end, we were selling thirty thousand a week on it.

JOE: The way you know is from the calls coming into the station; it might have sold only two hundred copies, but if people are calling the station, you know that it's got what it takes.

After "Just Out Of Reach," Jerry took on the job of shaping Solomon's career, with some help from a new producer, Bert Berns. "Sometime before this, Ahmet and I had stopped working together in the studio, because the thing had gotten too big, it got to the point where we had too many artists, and we split up the work, so I handled certain artists and he handled certain others.

"So then Bert Berns started coming around, he was a song plugger for Bobby Mellin getting fifty dollars a week, and he started showing me his material and I took a real fancy to him. I sensed he had a great talent, and I also liked him personally. He just came off the street one day, and started demonstrating songs to me, playing on guitar and piano, and he had so many ideas and licks, I said hey man, we're gonna produce some records together, because you're a producer. As a matter of fact, he had produced years before, some Latin things.

"One of the first songs that Bert brought us was 'Twist And Shout.' Atlantic had the first version of that, by Derek and Howard, we called them the Top something, the Top Notes. It was when Spector was working with us, and he and I produced the record and it was horrible.

Top: Estelle Axton and Jim Stewart, the sister and brother team who founded Stax Records in Memphis. Above: the Markeys, whose "Last Night" launched the label nationally.

Bert was such a newcomer, he was sitting in the spectators' booth, watching Phil and I butcher his song. Phil changed the middle around, we had the wrong tempo, the wrong feel, but we didn't realize that Bert could've produced it himself, and he just sat and watched us ruin it. Did he say anything afterward? Yeah, he said, 'Man, you fucked it up.'

"Anyway, I got to realize that Bert should co-produce, and one of the first things we did together was with Solomon Burke. I remember I introduced him to Solomon—and Bert was a real freaky guy to look at, with a long wig down his back, you know—and Solomon didn't say anything to him, but took me to one side, and said, 'C'mere, c'mon out in the hall,' where he says, 'Are you kiddin' me with this paddy motherfucker?' I says, 'Just be cool and listen to what he does, okay? Of course in ten minutes Solomon became enamored of him, and we're away to the races, cuttin' hits.

"One day a tape comes in from Detroit with eight songs on it. One of the songs was 'If You Need Me,' which was the only one that impressed me. So I take it along to Bert and say to him, 'I think this is a fantastic song for Solomon.' And he says, 'Yeah, it is, but what's wrong with the way it's done here?' The singer on the demo was Wilson Pickett.

"Now we had a policy at Atlantic, different from a lot of other companies, that we always looked after the artists we had. We've always looked for songs to build our artists. A lot of other companies would just take the artist and the song together, and drop the singer after the one hit. Chess, they did a lot of that, but we wouldn't do it. I would do anything to try to get the song and keep building the artist.

"So we recorded 'If You Need Me' with Solomon, and we felt we had a monster, and when we'd recorded it I had Robert West, who used to be manager of the Falcons, go up to Detroit with a personal check to Munro Golden for one thousand dollars for the publishing rights. But somebody, I don't know if it was one of our lawyers or what, neglected to get the rights to the demo in all the flurry and exchange of contracts." Without the rights to the original demo with Wilson Pickett, Atlantic had no way of preventing its release as competition for Solomon's version.

"So we've got the song in the can for Solomon, and one morning I get a phone call from Montagu [the disc jockey, the Magnificent Montagu], I'll never forget it, I was shaving at home in Great Neck, and he calls me and says, 'I've just got this master here that I've played seventeen times straight, it's unbelievable.' And I say, 'Who's the singer?' And he says, 'Wilson Pickett,' and I say, 'What's the song?' And he says, ' "If You Need Me," ' and I say, 'Oh no.'

"But I ask him who's got the master and he says Harold Logan and Lloyd Price.

"So I rush into the office and call in Logan and Price, and we have a big meeting. And we go around and around and around, and the only solution they would agree to is that I kill Solomon's record. They were favorably disposed toward Atlantic, they wanted us to distribute their master, but they wanted me to kill Solomon's record. I wanted to give them an interest in Solomon's record, and for them to give me the Pickett record and for me to hold it, maybe for future release.

"But there's no agreement, and they walk out, with Logan muttering. And they run to Liberty and get them to distribute it on their own Double L label.

"That record put me back into promotion. I went to work on that record, I was on the phone across the country. And I would say that Pickett's record had the edge over ours, but Liberty didn't know how to promote a record."

Pickett's record was on the *Billboard* chart for six weeks, and reached number 64; Burke's was there for eleven weeks, and made number 37.

"Later that year there was a convention down near Miami, and I walked into the lobby and there's Al Bennett, Liberty's president, standing with a group of people, and he kind of waved toward me, and said, 'People. Don't ever mess with this man.'

"The record got me back into the studio, back into the excitement of the record business, everything."

For a couple of years, Bert Berns was very important to Atlantic. In addition to rekindling Jerry's interest in producing, he took over the Drifters from Leiber and Stoller and produced a series of hits with them. But Bert was a producer in the old tradition, a man with epic symphonies in his head who liked to mold pliable singers and musicians. Probably only Phil Spector in Los Angeles and Jerry Ragavoy in Philadelphia, among his contemporary producers, could use so many instruments and such crescendos of sound without losing control of the effect they wanted to put across. But if the singer didn't want to fit his pattern, there could be irreconcilable conflicts. In 1965, Bert abandoned Solomon Burke to Jerry, who then found himself on his own.

"It got to the point where Bert couldn't work with Solomon anymore. We had a session due, and I said to Bert, 'Do you want to do this by yourself or should we do it together?' He said, 'I don't want to do it no way, baby, spare me, I can't stand the guy.'

"So I did it by myself, and we did 'Got To Get You Off My Mind,' 'Tonight's The Night,' and some more, I can't remember them. I called in Gene Page to arrange it—he'd done 'The In Crowd,' 'You've Lost That Lovin' Feelin'.' By the way, if you haven't noticed it, pay particular attention to the guitar obligato that runs all the way through

'Tonight's The Night,' it's by Eric Gale, who's a genius guitar player from New York."

The guitar playing is as impressive as Jerry remembers it, an electric blues solo winding itself around Solomon's husky, determined voice. And compared to Atlantic's first records with Solomon, the drumming is far more emphatic and "up" in the mix. But still the Atlantic sound was controlled, smooth, with all the spaces in the vocal closed up by a vocal group chanting choruses. Jerry has a feeling that in the long run, Solomon Burke might be acclaimed as the supreme soul singer of the sixties, ahead of current favorites like Otis Redding, James Brown, Bobby Bland, Joe Tex, and Wilson Pickett. In his day Solomon was superseded by singers who were less inhibited in the way they sang, more aggressive on fast songs and more impassioned on slow ones. Wilson Pickett, whose 'If You Need Me' had suffered in its fight with Solomon Burke's Atlantic version, was the singer who carried Atlantic—specifically Jerry Wexler—to the Southern Groove.

"Pretty soon after I started workin' with Solomon by myself, this must have been about a couple of years after 'If You Need Me,' Pickett himself comes into the office with a tape under his arm. He says, 'I'm through with those guys, I want to come home.' So I listen to the tape, a song that's about cryin'. And I said, 'Man, aren't you sore about what I did to you on "If You Need Me"?' And he said, 'That's in the past.' So I took a couple of his songs and put them out, but they didn't sell very well, round thirty thousand, forty thousand, and it's dues time, time to make a session. So I call Bert in, and say hey man, Pickett . . . and he says okay, and goes in and makes a very elaborate-sounding pop record, like a six thousand dollar session, and in those days you didn't spend that kind of money on a single. I listen to the record today, 'Come Home Baby,' and it's beautiful, Tami Lynn singing

Wilson Pickett. The search for a suitable musical framework for his harsh style led Jerry Wexler first to Memphis and then to Muscle Shoals, opening up the South to Atlantic.

obligato, but the record was a flop. Bert had Pickett crooning, something like Benny King sounded, and there really hadn't been any chemistry between them, there was too much going on in the studio. We were very much into using arrangers in those days.

"And we couldn't get it on. I'd play songs for him, and Pickett wouldn't like them, and vice versa. And I was thinking, we're gonna have to drop him. But then we got a call from his manager who says, 'Listen, we want to stay on Atlantic but you got to do something.' And that forced me to make a decision, and I got an idea: I called Jim Stewart in Memphis and said, 'Would you let me bring an artist down there, cut him in the studio with your band?' He said, sure. So I took Wilson down there, and opened up that southern thing for us."

MEMPHIS, TENNESSEE

Jim Stewart was the founder and owner of Stax Records, a Memphis-based label that Atlantic had been distributing nationally since 1960. Jerry made that 1960 arrangement, though he certainly had no idea of how productive it might be. He had heard about a record that was selling well in the Memphis area by a duo called Rufus and Carla, on the Satellite label. He instructed Atlantic's legal department to pick up national licensing rights, with options on any subsequent releases on the label. Rufus and Carla's "Deep Down Inside," which had been Satellite's second release, came out again on Atco but didn't sell as well nationwide as Jerry hoped. But "Gee Whiz" by Carla Thomas on her own, Satellite's fourth release, made the national top 10 when it was issued on Atlantic in 1961.

It was time to write a tighter contract. The people in Memphis evidently knew what they were doing in the studio, unlike many small-time independent southern producers who seemed to make commercial records almost by accident. Jim Stewart had ambitions to build his own label, and could not be satisfied with arrangements where he remained an independent producer issuing records on Atlantic's labels. To avoid confusion with a West Coast label called Satellite, Stewart changed his label's name to Stax, and committed his distribution and promotion to Atlantic. Since Carla Thomas was already contracted for release on the Atlantic label for two more years, her records, all produced in the Stax studios in Memphis, kept Atlantic's name in the charts. Meanwhile the Markeys, Booker T and and the M.G.s, William Bell, and Rufus Thomas (Carla's father, a local disc jockey) all had national hits on Stax during the first three years of the arrangement, 1961–63.

The success of this arrangement, which was consolidated over the following three years (1964–66), led to a significant restructuring of the whole record business, as other large independent companies took smaller companies under their wings. The arrangement protected them from the frequently long delays in receiving payment from independent record distributors, delays which often led to bankruptcy for these small companies who found themselves faced with bills from pressing plants before they received any income from records that had been sold.

Other companies already had comparable arrangements to the Atlantic-Stax deal, notably ABC-Paramount (who distributed Chancellor of Philadelphia), Mercury (various labels including Clock, in addition to many records licensed from smaller companies and issued on Mercury or its affiliate labels Smash or Philips), and King (DeLuxe of Linden, New Jersey, and Beltone of New York). But in

A Gold Record for Sam and Dave's "Soul Man," cele-brated by Jerry Wexler, Sam and Dave, Stax vice-president Al Bell, and Ahmet Ertegun. Inset: Stax president Jim Stewart.

most of these cases, the distributed label felt it was not getting proper attention from the parent organization, and sometimes not getting satisfactory statements either. Bel-tone Records of New York, who had a huge national hit in 1961 with Bobby Lewis' "Tossin' And Turnin'," sued King for $3,000,00 for overcharging on the record's press-ings and underpaying on sales. But relations between Stax and Atlantic, at least from 1961 to 1965 could not have been better. Stax made good records, Atlantic promoted and distributed them well, and paid Stax what they had contracted to pay.

The catalyst for the warmth between Memphis and New York was Otis Redding. Otis' career was an archetypal pop biography: a couple of early records in an untypical style, a few years of path-breaking recordings which did not sell outstandingly well, then a couple more years on a creative plateau, repeating effects but gathering acclaim, and finally a breakthrough to a new style, followed immediately by tragic death.

Otis was managed by Phil Walden, who took on the job as a sideline while he was still in college, with no intention of going into the music business full time. But Phil's sympathetic guidance was as important in the steady growth of Otis' career as Stax musicians or Atlantic promotion. Within a few years, not only was Otis among the best paid R and B singers in the country, but the Walden management agency had taken on representation of many of the most successful southern R and B singers, including Sam and Dave, Percy Sledge, Johnnie Taylor, Eddie Floyd, and William Bell. But whereas with most of the other singers, Phil's relationship was strictly business, with little love lost between singer and agent, with Otis it was different, says Phil. "I loved him, but it really wasn't good to get that close. When it ends, the feeling is too strong. I used to feel really excited when Otis would introduce me and say, 'This is my manager.' I didn't know anything when I started, but I was anxious to learn and I did, fast.

"There was no tradition of southern management agencies, they were all in New York, but we got to be the biggest R and B booking agency in the world—we were surprised when we looked around and saw how big we were.

"The first tour I ever did was called the Hot Summer

Review—Otis Redding, Joe Tex, the Fiestas, Bobby Marchan, Eddie Kirkland, and a band—that went out for seven hundred and fifty dollars a night. We all went on a bus, stayed in colored motels, Otis and I always stayed in the same bed, if he was balling a chick I was just lying there.

"We once got Otis booked into the Royal Peacock in Atlanta, one hundred and fifty dollars for three days. We went up there and took one hundred of it and bought him a mohair suit. The hotel we stayed at had pictures up front saying Little Richard stayed here, Fats Domino stayed here, so I said shit, we gotta stay here too. It was about two dollars a night, and man it was really beat up, the bed touched the floor when you laid on it. Of course I could have afforded to stay somewhere a little better, but I was all for getting in there, you know, sharing the life that Otis lived."

The first Otis Redding record to have any impact was "These Arms of Mine," released on the newly formed Stax subsidiary, Volt, in 1963. But three other records were involved in the pre-history of that session. The first was the record that Bobby Robinson remembers being sent from Georgia, "Shout Bamalama" by Otis on the Confederate label. Bobby's judgment had been accurate: "Shout Bamalama" didn't sell until Otis became famous, when everything with his name on it acquired catalogue value, including that imitation of Little Richard and an even worse thing called "She's Alright," which Otis recorded during a stay of a few months in California. On "She's Alright" Otis imitated Barret Strong, recently in the charts with "Money."

The third pre-history record, "Love Twist," wasn't by Otis at all, but a group called Johnny Jenkins' Pinetoppers. First issued on a small Georgia label, it was picked up by Atlantic on the advice of their southern promotion man Joe Galkin. It didn't sell many copies, but Galkin wanted to do another session with the group, using the Stax studios. Joe traced the publisher of "Love Twist" to Phil Walden in Macon, Georgia. Phil, it turned out, was not only a publisher, but the manager of Johnny Jenkins and Otis Redding. Phil suggested that if Joe was planning to cut a record with Johnny, he should take Otis along too, and cut something with him. Joe was sure that he didn't want to make any record with Otis Redding. According to Joe:

"I told Phil, he's a lousy singer. Otis had made a record called 'Shout Bamalama' down there in Athens, Georgia, that was the worst record I ever heard. It had got plays on WLAC with John Richbourg, but nobody ever bought a copy."

But Phil was an effective talker, and despite Joe's objections, Phil persuaded him to take Otis up to Memphis, even if it was just to drive the rented station wagon that was carrying the Pinetoppers to the session.

Phil made sure that Otis got to Memphis, but he wasn't at the recording session to insist that Otis have a chance to sing, and in the end it was Joe Galkin who stood up for Otis. Joe watched the session with rising alarm as Johnny Jenkins and the Pinetoppers failed to play anything worth recording. "After about two and a half hours, Jim Stewart, who was producing and engineering the Pinetoppers' session for us [Atlantic], said 'Joe, I cannot make a record with this group,' so I didn't want to waste the last half hour of studio time and I said, 'Okay, then let's do something with this guy, Otis Redding, he's a singer.' Steve Cropper and Al Jackson were ready to walk out, and Jim and I argued back and forth; he says 'What'll you give me,' and I said 'fifty percent of the publishing right.' So Otis cuts 'These Arms Of Mine,' and 'Hey Hey

Otis Redding, pensive and in action. He not only developed a very effective style of interpretation that opened up the previously resistant "white rock" market to R&B, but through his engaging offstage personality he generated an unprecedented loyalty towards himself and the whole "Stax-Atlantic" sound from fans and even record company staff.

Baby.' Well Jim didn't think too much of them, so he gave his part of the songs away to John Richbourg up in Nashville, Tennessee, at WLAC. And John started wailing on the record, and another guy in Memphis, Hamp Sway, went on it too, and it sold. But Jim waited another eight months before he cut another record by Otis. Eight months."

Although technically it was an Atlantic session that recorded Otis, Jim Stewart was allowed to release Otis on his new Volt label. Atlantic got the first album on Atco, and also recorded Otis on a live album, *Saturday Night At The Apollo*. The show at the Apollo was Otis' first appearance there. It followed two substantial R and B hits, "These Arms Of Mine" and "Pain In My Heart," but according to Phil Walden Otis got paid only $400 for the week.

"It cost him that much to get up there and live in New York for a week. He went up by bus, with the only two suits he owned. He said to the girl next to him on the bus, 'Have you heard "These Arms Of Mine,"' and she said, 'Oh yeah, I like it,' and he said, 'I made it, and "Pain In My Heart,"' and she said, 'So what are you doing on a bus?'"

The MC at the Apollo seemed to know what was coming, though. After Wilson Pickett and the Falcons had broken the audience up with typically searing gospel-based songs, the announcer calmed them down. "You ain't seen nothin' yet, Sapphire. I got somethin' else for you, mama, this guy here's making his first appearance at the Apollo and he can *sing*, baby, he can *sing*—Otis Redding." And as Otis drew his first breath, a girl in the audience called out, "Sing it pretty now, Otis." He did.

Jerry Wexler and Tommy Dowd, who were there to record the show, must have been impressed with Otis' effect on the audience, despite his apparent ignorance of even the basic principles of how to project himself and his material on stage. "He just stood there and sang," recalled Rufus Thomas, a fellow Stax artist who was on the same bill and who tried to teach Otis how to walk onto the stage and what to do with his hands while he was singing.

The singles which followed at regular intervals during the next eighteen months sold quite well, without establishing Otis Redding as a major name—he was competing with the Motown hit factory at its most effective, and the British group invasion at its most hysterical. In the early spring of 1965, Tommy Dowd went down to Memphis to see if he could help in the studio. Although he doesn't reckon he offered much—"Those guys knew what they were doing, and worked very well together"—the breakthrough came from records made at that session, the single "I've Been Loving You Too Long," and the album *Otis Blue,* which spawned two more American hits, "Respect" and "Satisfaction," and his first British hit, "My Girl." Even these records failed to reach the top 20 in *Billboard*'s national pop chart, but they established him as a name that disc jockeys and fans started to look out for.

Soon after Tom Dowd had been welcomed to the Stax studios Jerry went to Memphis with Wilson Pickett—July 1965. Jerry had attended sessions at Stax before, and watched the staff work on a Carla Thomas record, but had not made any constructive suggestions himself. But this time, he made contributions which were noticed, effective, and appreciated, as Jann Wenner discovered when three years later he went to interview the musicians involved, guitarist and composer Steve Cropper, drummer Al Jackson, and bassist Duck Dunn, for *Rolling Stone.*

Steve Cropper talked most: "Somebody came up and says, 'Hey, write a tune for Wilson, he's coming in and we've got to produce Wilson Pickett.' . . . We didn't want to write ballad stuff because the rock beat was happening then. I grabbed the only album of his I could find in the studio, which was two or three cuts which he did at the Apollo and at the end of each fade-out he'd say, 'Yeah, wait for the midnight hour, baby.' . . . I thought that would be a heck of an idea for a tune, and when he came in I presented it to him, and he said that's a good idea and he said, 'I've got this little rhythm thing I've been working on for a good while.' There was really nothing to it, it was just a couple of changes and we just started working with this. That was where it came from.

"When I wrote the tune I had it going a completely different way. Basically the changes were the same, basic feel was the same, but there was a different color about it. During the session Jerry said, 'Why don't you pick up on this thing here?' He said this was the way the kids were dancing, they were putting the accent on two. Basically, we have been one beat accenters with an after-beat, it was like 'boom dah,' but here this was a thing that went 'un-chaw,' just the reverse as far as the accent goes. The back beat was somewhat delayed and it just put it in that rhythm, and Al and I have been using that as a natural thing now, ever since we did it. We play a downbeat and then two is just almost on but a little bit behind only with complete impact. It turned us on to a heck of a thing."

AL: It was different.

STEVE: There's lots of things involved in this song. The bass line is a tremendous bass line. I came up with most of the horn lines, but the horn players do a hell of a job on the thing. It was a good feeling session, and out of that session of "The Midnight Hour" there were four hit singles. "Don't Fight It" was another big record. . . . "I'm Not Tired," that slow blues with a beat . . . and "It's A Man's Way." . . .

Inset: the most famous rhythm section in pop history, clockwise from left: Booker T (organ), Al Jackson, Jr (drums), Steve Cropper (guitar) and Duck Dunn (bass). Above: Steve Cropper's spare rhythm guitar style was enormously influential for the next twenty years.

DUCK: Well the bass thing was really Jerry Wexler's idea. Like Steve said, we had it going another way. Jerry came out and did the jerk dance.

STEVE: Yeah, that's where he got it from. We had the funk but he knew what the kids were doing.

JANN: Jerry came out of the booth and started dancing?

DUCK: To the jerk.

STEVE: Yeah, he actually came out and said, "Do it this way, this is the way they're doing it."

AL: To tell you really, you wouldn't believe the way it was played on the floor and the way it is now. When I would count the tune off, Duck [on bass] would stay where I counted it. He was playing the top and Steve and I were playing the middle. It sounded really as though the two and four were late. It was so far behind that you wouldn't believe it, and how it came out like this, we don't know. Then it became natural for Steve and I to play the delayed two-four after that.

JANN: Did Jerry's coming down to do this tune make that great a change of direction?

AL: To me it did.

STEVE: I think it did. I think it was the first time we had a chance to work with somebody that was up on the music scene from a different part of the country. We had been doing our own kind of thing, the way we wanted to do it.

The Stax sound really dates from that session. Eddie Floyd's "Knock On Wood," Sam and Dave's "Hold On, I'm A-Coming," and Don Covay's "See Saw" all have a similar feeling to "The Midnight Hour," both in the way the rhythm drives the listener's body, and in the scansion of the vocal lines. But although Jerry had helped to give Stax a formula for even more commercial success than they had already enjoyed, undercurrents of resentment began to surface after the Pickett sessions, sometime around 1966. Perhaps Jim Stewart felt that since Wilson Pickett used the Stax sound, he should have been on the Stax label; or maybe he thought that Atlantic should have paid a higher royalty per Stax record sold. Whatever the basis for disagreement, no more artists recorded in the Stax studio for the Atlantic label after the Pickett sessions. When Jerry signed up Sam and Dave and wanted to use Memphis musicians on their records, he had to put them on the Stax label.

By this time the Southern Groove had proved itself a genuine commercial commodity, and Stax was out to milk its new popularity for all it could get. Sam and Dave's "Soul Man" made number 2 on the *Billboard* chart in the fall of 1967, the highest position yet for a record on Stax. Then Otis had a fatal air crash, and his "Dock Of The Bay" made number 1 posthumously early in 1968. Later that year, Stax withdrew from the distribution deal with Atlantic, and entered into one with Gulf-Western. Stax had a big hit soon after moving to Gulf-Western, Johnnie Taylor's "Who's Making Love," but the proceeds from that were quickly dissipated in a flood-the-market-with-product policy that forced too many hastily produced albums on an understandably disinterested public. Staving off disaster through the peculiar success of monologue/ballad albums by Isaac Hayes, Stax rescued itself by buying out of the contract with Gulf-Western with a loan from Polydor of two million dollars, in immediate return for which Polydor took international licensing rights to their product. Widely credited with holding the company together through this rough period, Stax vice-president Al Bell freely acknowledges Jerry Wexler as his mentor.

Al Bell joined Stax at Jerry's suggestion, when Jim Stewart thought that Stax ought to build up its own production staff to back up Atlantic's. Jerry recommended Al, then a rhythm and blues disc jockey in Washington, D.C., and offered to pay half his salary until Stax could afford to cover it all. A big, charismatic figure, Al praises Jerry like a man making a speech at a testimonial dinner. "Jerry

Wexler is one of the greatest, if not the greatest, man in the record business. If it had not been for Jerry Wexler, there would have been no Stax Records, no Al Bell. Jerry Wexler taught me all I know about the record business today. We used to speak on the phone on Saturday mornings, matching thoughts about what had happened during the week. I wanted to know, and Jerry was not afraid to tell me, he wasn't afraid that I represented competition to him. And that's why Jerry will be successful, because the people he helped are always there, at his beck and call. He could call me and say, 'Al, I have to have ...' and he would get it. So long as it didn't jeopardize anybody's life, anything like that.

"He did it. He opened the door for black artists, banged on the door and wouldn't take no for an answer."

This was always the word on Jerry Wexler: that he opened up opportunities for black performers in pop music, especially those who sang in a black idiom, who didn't try to disguise the gospel or blues roots of their style. Yet although most of the people he was ever associated with were very quick to find kind words for him, the majority of them eventually declined to go on doing business with him. As southerners seem to see him, Jerry Wexler is too demanding, or too clever, or too narrowminded. They agree that he made invaluable contributions to their success, yet they are nagged by the feeling that somehow he got more from their efforts than they did. Several southern producers have opted for a more anonymous relationship, with companies like CBS, Capitol, MGM, or Bell, whose administrators leave creative decisions in the hands of the producers. Recently, Stax made yet another move in its attempts to set up a secure business, this time arranging distribution through CBS, a company with huge financial resources but limited experience in promoting rhythm and blues music.

Steve Cropper, the guitarist whose gentle, precise flicks gave character to the smooth rolling rhythm of "Green Onions" by Booker T and the M.G.s, is one of the Memphis musicians who preferred not to work with Jerry. The M.G.s ("Memphis Group") were the Stax house rhythm section, and Steve played guitar on most of the studio's records, often contributing a decisive melodic phrase which qualified him for co-authorship credits. He graduated to the role of producer, worked long hours and earned enough to open a studio of his own in 1970, freelancing for various companies including Stax, and producing for his own TMI label which he entrusted to the CBS distribution and promotion system. He agreed that Atlantic would have been a more obvious choice for distribution.

"But I didn't want to go into competition with what I'd been doing there. If I'd gone with Atlantic, I felt I'd have been forced into the position where I'd have been asked to produce Wilson Pickett, Don Covay, create another Otis Redding. As far as I'm concerned, those days have gone. I'm tired of living in the past. And Clive Davis at Columbia did not make specifications. If I say a record is going to be a hit, they will get behind it. I'm not criticizing Jerry Wexler, I'm describing the way he works. If I handed him an R and B record and he didn't like it, he'd send it back and say I should do this or that; but Columbia don't question my judgment."

The rejections and rebuffs from Memphis which began back in 1965 depressed Jerry, but he also realized that the Stax studios weren't the only place with a good rhythm section capable of playing the Southern Groove. There was a studio called Fame, not far away in Muscle Shoals,

Alabama, which had a sound that was just as good, if not better. Early in 1966, he took Wilson Pickett there.

MUSCLE SHOALS, ALABAMA

Unlike Memphis, Muscle Shoals has no great tradition of music making. Memphis is perfectly placed, geographically, to mix the heavy, emotional music of people coming north from Louisiana and Mississippi with the more melodic and sweet music of local country people. Memphis was a music center in the twenties and thirties, and then again during the fifties when it spawned one of the strongest rock 'n' roll styles in the studios of Sun Records—where Elvis Presley, Jerry Lee Lewis and several others brought country and boogie, blues and ballads together. The Stax musicians, some of them black (notably drummer Al Jackson and keyboard player Booker T Jones) but most of them white (Steve Cropper, and the horn section), had absorbed the numerous sounds and styles available on the radio, and several of them made their debuts as session musicians during the declining years of the Sun studios.

The Muscle Shoals sound, in contrast, is strictly the result of one man's industry and persistence, Rick Hall of the Fame studios. After some years touring locally with a four-piece combo, occasionally doing session work at the Hi studios in Memphis and writing songs in partnership with Billy Sherrill, Rick opened the Fame studios in 1961 in Florence, Alabama, where he lived. The association of the studio with Muscle Shoals has probably resulted from the fact that when people fly to record there, they land at Muscle Shoals Airport, which services the three adjacent towns of Florence, Sheffield, and Muscle Shoals.

Although the expression "Muscle Shoals sound" is freely used, it is not that readily identifiable a style. It is difficult to say, on hearing a particular record, that it was recorded at Fame, that Rick Hall was the producer, arranger, or engineer, or that his unit of musicians was playing. In contrast to the studio group at Stax and Hi in Memphis, almost all of the regular Muscle Shoals musicians were white, but as they all preferred to play rhythm and blues, it's hard to distinguish their sound from a Memphis rhythm and blues record. On slow numbers, Muscle Shoals arrangements tended to be more "churchy," with piano or organ conjuring images of heads bowed in humble dedication—Percy Sledge's "When A Man Loves A Woman" is a definitive example. On fast ones, Rick Hall's trademark was to have a particular riff on guitar repeated throughout a song, a clever subliminal device which quickly established a listener's familiarity with the record which on the surface might seem to be very similar to a number of other fast dance records.

The reputation of most producers is based not so much on a consistent, identifiable style, but on how they are tuned in to current tastes and whether they have a disciplined session group and team of writers who can be relied upon to turn out a "commercial product." In ten years, Rick Hall has risen to the top of this list, and although much of his success has had not evident connection to Atlantic, Jerry Wexler came in at a crucial time in Rick's career and so provided the stability and self-confidence which led to greater success later.

Although Rick's bias toward rhythm and blues isn't so strong as that of the Stax musicians and producers or even his own musicians, most of his early success was with black singers. His first hit came with Arthur Alexander in 1962. "Arthur was a bellhop here, in a small hotel. I cut him doing one of his own songs, "You Better Move On," a low budget thing that must have cost about five hundred dollars. I sold the master to Dot, and it was a smash. And then Bill Lowery came here, he was really the first man to believe in Muscle Shoals as a place to record."

Bill Lowery was a publisher who refused to move his offices from Atlanta, Georgia, to Nashville or New York, and developed an extraordinary stable of writers who all came from the Atlanta area. "Young Love" in 1957 and "Walk On By" in 1961 were isolated early hits, but from 1963 onward he had an apparently endless succession by his own writers and singers, including Joe South, Jerry Reed, Ray Stevens, Ray Whitney, Tommy Roe, Billy Joe Royal, and the Tams. One of Lowery's producers, Felton Jarvis, won one of pop music's most coveted positions when he became Elvis Presley's producer in the mid-sixties. But curiously, although Lowery built up an efficient publishing organization, he was never able to launch a successful record company, despite several attempts. Fairlane (distributed by King), Allwood (which Atlantic distributed), and NRC (self-distributed) were among the labels run by Lowery's organization or in conjunction with Bert Woodall, that all folded after only a year or so. But while these labels struggled, Lowery's writers and singers had hits on larger labels, often engineered and produced by Rick Hall. According to Rick, "Bill started coming here after NRC Records had gone bankrupt in Atlanta. We'd become friends in Nashville, but he didn't like the stereotyped, cut-and-dried, rimp-shimp, rimp-shimp, doo-doo-doot kind of thing, like me, so he wanted to get away from that and brought his singers to me to record."

While Lowery provided the singers and the songs, Rick collected the musicians, mostly from groups playing locally in clubs and bars. Among the first musicians he used was an entire band called Dan Penn and the Pallbearers, who adopted their name after buying a hearse for transporting the band. Dan Penn, a singer and song writer who at the age of 14 had provided Conway Twitty with a national hit, "Is A Bluebird Blue," became a very important source of material for Rick, while David Briggs (piano), Norbert Putnam (bass), and Jerry Carrigan (drums) became the

Left: Albert King; right: Rufus Thomas, Jr. These two veterans had both been recording since the early fifties, but enjoyed the greatest success of their careers during the mid-sixties with Stax.

regular session group. All three musicians later moved to Nashville, where they soon joined the small ranks of elite session men who could work virtually nonstop, day after day, capable of adjusting to virtually any style. To outsiders it seemed that Rick had lost the backbone of his business with the departure of Penn's group, but he found other musicians. These replacements left in turn to work on their own, making way for new recruits; it became apparent that Rick had a flair for choosing good musicians, and for giving them invaluable training, then letting them go when they asserted some independence. His principle seems to have been to record incessantly, or anyway for as long as the money lasted.

Rick's studio provided hits for Bill Lowery with the Tams (including "Untie Me," written by Joe South, and "What Kind Of Fool Do You Think I Am," written by Ray Whitney), and with Tommy Roe ("Everybody," a top 10 hit in 1963 on ABC). "It was a one-man operation," Rick recalled, "I charged twenty-five dollars an hour, all in mono, and I cleaned up the studio, engineered the dates, wrote the letters." In 1964, he formed his own label, Fame, and immediately came up with a hit, "Steal Away" by Jimmy Hughes. But he had trouble getting it off the ground.

At first, he was prepared to lease "Steal Away" to another label, but nobody would take it. "I took it to everybody I knew in Nashville, but they said it was too R and B. So I called Bill Lowery and said what do you think about my putting it out on my own label. He said go ahead, but make sure you ship it C.O.D.

"So I had some pressed, and I put them in my car and I drove in a big circle, from here to Memphis, stayed there a night, then to Little Rock, from there to Shreveport, on to Baton Rouge, to New Orleans, Mobile, Montgomery, Birmingham and back up here. I bought a case of whiskey, vodka, or some kind of drink, and I gave each of the disc jockeys a bottle. And they started playing the fire out of 'Steal Away.'

"So I call up Kesslers, the distributors in Memphis, and say did you get any calls on a record called 'Steal Away'? And they said, yeah, send us six hundred and fifty, which meant they would buy five hundred and I had to give them one hundred and fifty free. If you figure that out, if means you have to give away three hundred thousand to sell a million. So I said, well I can't do that unless you give me C.O.D. And they said okay. And I called each of the distributors in the areas I'd been to, and got the same answer. And the next week it had gone up to thirteen hundred. And in a few weeks, the whole country was after it, but I couldn't do it by myself. So I called Bill Lowery again, and he said, Steve Clark, vice-president of Vee Jay, is a friend of mine, take it there.

"Vee Jay offered me ten thousand dollars in front, which was a lot of money for me then, plus eight or nine percent I think. The record sold about eight hundred and fifty thousand. And I started producing some records for Vee Jay; we did Joe Simon's 'My Adorable One,' and Dan Penn's song 'Let's Do It Over.'"

Next to come along, in the fall of 1964, was Nashville producer Buddy Killen, with Joe Tex. Buddy and Joe had been working together for two or three years in Nashville without ever getting a national hit. In 1964, Killen switched distribution of his Dial label from London to Atlantic and took Joe—and the band he'd already been recording with—to Rick Hall's studio. The first record under this new arrangement brought Joe Tex his first hit, the sermonizing "Hold What You've Got." Several more followed.

The Fame studios at Muscle Shoals began to gather a reputation within the industry, but the Fame label was set back when Vee Jay went bankrupt in 1965, leaving Rick with no distribution. Rick called Jerry Wexler, who agreed to add Fame to the growing roster of independent labels distributed by Atlantic. And the real breakthrough for Muscle Shoals came when Jerry went there himself, to produce Wilson Pickett.

Jerry was knocked out by the musicians at Fame. The original Pallbearers session men had already gone to Nashville by the time Jerry got there in 1966, but their successors were at least as good in Jerry's opinion. "The rhythm section I used there was Chips Moman on guitar, Tommy Cogbill on bass, Spooner Oldham on keyboards,

*At left: Joe Tex, a regular hit-maker since
"Hold What You've Got" in 1964, signs auto-
graphs for some fans. At right: Percy Sledge,
whose "When A Man Loves A Woman" was in many
ways the definitive Muscle Shoals record, and
a vital influence on the "pastoral" rock of
Procol Harum, Traffic, and The Band.*

Roger Hawkins on drums—the greatest drummer in the
world, still—and Jimmy Johnson on rhythm guitar. And
do you know, Rick Hall didn't know that Tommy could
play bass! He was playing third guitar, and Junior Lowe
was playing bass and just not cutting it, and Chips comes
up to me and says, 'Hey, Tommy can play bass, let's give
him a try.' Rick had never bothered to find out what else
he could do. And Tommy became a master session bass
player.

"The trouble with Rick is that he's too authoritarian in

the studio, he treats his musicians like shit. He says he doesn't depend on musicians, and if they don't like working with him, he can get somebody else."

Rick Hall doesn't contest this account of his approach. "Jerry thinks that musicians are the answer to hit records. I say musicians are like basketball players, they need a manager to tell them when to drop a play. My engineering ability and advice on licks and beats contributes more than the individual musicians." Rick extends this attitude into what might be considered a rather ruthless method of paying his men. He prefers to pay them for each piece of work rather than put them on a regular salary, and so keep them hungry, deny them security. He feels his results justify his methods.

"I must have done a hundred and fifty songs with Dan Penn and Spooner Oldham, and I bought each one, it probably cost me fifty thousand dollars to buy them. Somebody else would have put them under contract with a yearly salary, and it would have worked out cheaper. But to me when they're hungry and on the way up, they're starting to be someone; but if they get there, that's it, they start partying, and may never write any more hits." It's certainly true that Dan Penn wrote more effective songs when he was with Rick—for James Carr, Joe Simon, Percy Sledge, and others—than he has since. But on the other hand, Rick may have lost a lot of royalties on one of the biggest Muscle Shoals hits, "When A Man Loves A Woman," by refusing to put his people on salary.

"634-5789," Wilson Pickett's first Muscle Shoals record, with Jerry as producer and Rick as engineer, was a respectable hit early in 1966, but when 'When A Man Loves A Woman" was recorded shortly afterward, neither Rick nor Jerry was around. Quin Ivy, one of the writers who supplied song material to Rick, and Marlin Greene, a session musician and composer, had discovered a local gospel-styled singer, Percy Sledge. They recorded Percy's "When A Man Loves A Woman" in a makeshift studio near Muscle Shoals using Rick's regular (but uncontracted) session musicians. Not knowing how to get the tape to a record company, Quin and Marlin then took it to Rick, who recommended that they send it to Atlantic, for which service he earned himself a royalty on every record sold. It wasn't anything compared to what he would have received had he recorded the record himself, but since the record sold well over a million, becoming the first southern soul record to top the pop chart, the royalties were still considerable, and helped Rick to clear his debts on his studio at the same time as it enabled the owners of the "Quinvy" studio to equip themselves with modern gadgetry.

Through 1966, the Fame studios became steadily busier, as both Wilson Pickett and Percy Sledge sustained a series of successful records, and attracted other customers. In February 1967 Jerry Wexler came to produce another singer for perhaps the most significant session he was ever involved in, the session that resulted in Aretha Franklin's "I Never Loved A Man (The Way I Loved You)." Daughter of a Detroit preacher, Aretha had made some gospel records for a small Chicago label, JVB, which revealed that even in her teens she was an intensely emotional, idiosyncratic, but accurate singer, and an atmospheric pianist too. She was contracted to Columbia at the instigation of John Hammond, whose work as a producer of jazz and blues for Columbia since the mid-1930s made him one of the few men in the music business that Jerry Wexler unreservedly admired. For eight years, Columbia recorded Aretha in every guise they could think of, singing standards, pop songs, with jazz-styled accompaniments, even doing current R and B hits. They made nine LPs, countless singles, accumulated a loss of $90,000, and had two minor hits. When her contract came up for renewal, Atlantic moved in, signed her up, and told the music world that at last the real Aretha Franklin would be revealed. It was a rare opportunity for Atlantic to prove it was a company whose senior staff knew how to make records, to throw a stone in Goliath's eye. "With that record," said Shirley Wexler, "Jerry felt like he was on stage. Everybody was watching him."

Although Jerry had sorted out a number of songs that he thought Aretha might like to do during her first session—which would be for a complete album, although a single would come out of it—Aretha had found "I Never Loved A Man" herself. In the studio, Jerry recalled, "she played it to the rhythm section, Charlie Chalmers went into Rick's office to write out the horn parts, and when he came back out with the arrangement, we played the whole band together. There are no overdubs on that record. Spooner plays electric piano, Aretha stays out for the first eight bars. Oh yeah, we did overdub her voice double tracking on the long open break—that was Chips Moman's idea."

Jerry had planned to stay in Muscle Shoals with Aretha for a week, but after only one day they were on the plane back to New York. Nobody likes to talk about what happened, but it's clear that Aretha's husband, Ted White, was the chief source of friction, as he was to be for the next few years until he and Aretha separated. For a session that had been supposed to prove to the world how Atlantic made records, the Muscle Shoals trip apparently had been a disaster. Clutched under his arm, Jerry had one complete tape of "I Never Loved A Man," and a three-piece track of a song called "Do Right Woman—Do Right Man."

"Dan Penn and Chips Moman gave us that song while we were in the studio; as a matter of fact, they hadn't

Aretha Franklin. What Ray Charles had been in the fifties, Aretha became for the sixties, a piano-playing singer and arranger with an intuitive sense of the ultimate approach to a song. But whereas Ray Charles' records had been mostly confined to the R&B market, Aretha's "went pop" from the start.

finished it, they were stuck at the bridge, and I gave them a couple of lines that broke the jam. It was still in the typewriter when we were ready to cut it.

"When we got back to New York I had some acetates cut on 'I Never Loved A Man.' I was very excited about it. I got on the phone and started playing it for all the black disc jockeys that I knew well enough to call on a Sunday, and that was quite a few. The reaction was incredible. So I sent out some dubs, but I didn't have a B side, and they started playing the thing and I couldn't press the record. All I had on 'Do Right Woman' was guitar, drums, and bass. And I couldn't get Aretha back into a studio for about a week. But I did finally get her in, with her two sisters, that's all we had. And she put piano and organ on herself, and then she, Carolyn, and Erma did the vocal parts."

The final 45 was a masterpiece of emotion, musicianship, and control, and, maybe more important, it made the top 10. After ten years, Aretha had finally made it. Her next seven singles also made the top 10, so that a "failure," commercially, was her version of The Band's "The Weight," which only made number 19 on *Billboard,* or "Eleanor Rigby," which stopped at number 17. "When Aretha records a tune," King Curtis commented, "she kills a copyright. Because once she's worked out the way to do it, you're never going to be able to come up with a better approach. And it's damn sure you're not going to be able to improve on how she's done it, her way."

Dear Mr. Wexler, I'm Aretha's number one fan and you should stop having her record all this shit like "Eleanor Rigby." Next thing, we'll have to put up with her singing, "I am Mrs. Robinson." This letter was one of Ahmet's practical jokes, but he had to wait two years before he could shove a gentle spoke in his partner's wheels. Nothing that Jerry had done with the Drifters or Ray Charles could have prepared Ahmet, or anybody else who knew him, for that extraordinary success with Aretha, which brought Jerry the music industry's award for Best Producer two years in a row. And although the rate slowed down during 1969 and 1970, when none of Aretha's records cracked *Billboard's* top 10, she came back in 1971 with "Bridge Over Troubled Water"/"Brand New Me," which came close to three million copies in combined sales. And although Atlantic's success with soul had seemed to depend on southern rhythm sections and studios, most of Aretha's hits were cut in New York, sometimes with southern musicians flown up for her sessions, but also with New York session men coordinated by King Curtis, probably the most versatile and sympathetic accompanist of his era. When Atlantic's staff found it difficult to communicate with Aretha, even to persuade her to come to the studio to make a record or rehearse a new song, Curtis was the in-between man who soothed and persuaded her; when he was fatally stabbed outside his apartment late in 1971, Atlantic and the entire record business lost one of the most important figures of contemporary music.

Ironically, Curtis had preferred to stay in New York and record in local studios with local musicians, rather than go south. He did make some records at American Group Productions (AGP) in Memphis, but he had no desire to return when interviewed six months before he was killed. "I was in Memphis last week, you stay in the studio till eleven o'clock and when you come out you can't even get anything to eat. It's a little inconvenient down there. In the South, you have to restrain yourself to make sure you come back alive. And I don't need to go to Miami or Muscle Shoals to record, because I can find what I want right here."

True enough, Curtis in New York put together one of the finest session groups of any time, with Richard Tee on piano, Cornell Dupree on guitar, Jerry Jemmott on bass, and Bernard Purdie on drums. But despite the exceptional combination of virtuosity and versatility which the musicians displayed on Aretha's later Atlantic records (with Aretha on piano in place of Tee), Jerry went back south for both dance "groove" records and for polished commercial arrangements.

There were two motives for working with southern musicians. One, it was enjoyable to work with them, since they were so flexible and prepared to try out new ideas. Two, a question of money. In New York, musicians worked strictly to union rates, scales, and terms. A three-hour period in the studio constituted a session, and the musicians got paid according to how many three-hour units they worked. If there were difficulties in finding a suitable arrangement for a song, a record could be very expensive to make in New York. If the problem was with the drum part, and the other musicians simply sat around for a day while it was straightened out, everybody had to be paid. Economics dictated that in New York it was best to have an arrangement ready before a session started, and to use musicians who could read music. After three hours, a producer would be inclined to settle for the best take he had made at that point, even if it did not represent what he had been hoping for. These conditions didn't lead to much spontaneous interplay between musicians, and it was in search of such interplay that Jerry went south.

The southern musicians were generally prepared to stretch union definitions of what a session was, working on one song for as long as it took to get the right feel, accepting that one session was a song rather than a three-hour unit of time.

In 1967, not long after the first Aretha sessions, Chips Moman led another "migration" of session musicians out of Rick Hall's Fame studios, this time to Memphis, where Chips and Tommy Cogbill started the American Group

The bottom of the Muscle Shoals sound: bass player David Hood and drummer Roger Hawkins ("the best in the world," according to Jerry Wexler), pictured when they were enrolled into the British rock group Traffic for an American tour in 1972.

Productions (AGP) recording studio. Almost immediately they produced a national number 1, "The Letter" by the Box Tops, which was followed by several more hits for the group. Jerry had not only encouraged Chips and Tommy to believe in their own talent when they were working for Rick Hall, but had lent $5,000 to Chips for an indeterminate period with no security. The next thing he knew, Chips signed a production deal with Larry Utall, the owner of Bell Records, who was in the process of setting up a distributing network that was evidently modeled on what Jerry had intuitively developed at Atlantic. "I never heard from Chips," Jerry complained. "When he got the Box Tops, I never got a call from him, hey, I got something for you, no, he went every place else."

But Jerry didn't let his hurt feelings interfere with his hearing, which recognized in AGP another studio with an instinct for a good groove. He recommended that King Curtis use the AGP band, and took British singer Dusty Springfield there in 1968 to record the very tasteful album *Dusty in Memphis*. The Memphis sessions spawned several hit 45s, notably "Son Of A Preacher Man" with its liquid southern guitar licks not previously familiar to the young pop fans who constituted Dusty's main audience. Not long afterward, Elvis Presley went to record at the same studio for his first sessions in Memphis since 1955. There was a curious "Atlantic" feeling to the songs he cut there, in particular "In The Ghetto" and "Suspicious Minds," the latter with vocal backing from Atlantic's act the Sweet Inspirations.

But even though it seemed that half the pop music industry was breathing down Jerry's neck, copying every move he made in the hope of catching the same magic, Jerry did not become defensive or secretive. "I've always had what might be considered an anomalous attitude, that whatever I've come into, I've not wanted to keep it all to myself. I've never been afraid of somebody coming in and stealing my lick, or my riff, or my sound, if I have one. Because they can't do it. They could take you tomorrow and drop you down in the Motown studios with all the apparatus, all the gear, and you wouldn't be able to come up with a Motown record. They could say, here's the blueprint, here's how you do it—but still you couldn't. That's why I think it's unnecessary for anybody who's making it to be paranoid about guarding their professional secrets.

"People would say, 'Who was that guitar player on your last Pickett record?' and we'd say, 'Here, here's his phone number.' And we've always done that. We've never signed exclusives on people.

"But once a guy I didn't know called me up—I knew his name but I'd never met him—and said, 'Hey Jerry, how do you go about cutting a record in Muscle Shoals?' And I must have been in an evil mood, because I said, 'I'll tell you what to do. You go down to Kennedy and take the Delta Airlines to Memphis; change to Southern and get off at Muscle Shoals. Find a yellow pages and look under "studios." Because that's how I did it, motherfucker.' But a couple of hours later, I called him up and gave him Jimmy Johnson's phone number. I don't know why people expect us to give them all the answers, but the funny thing is, we do."

But although Jerry has undoubtedly performed an immeasurable service for southern music, by demonstrating that virtually any kind of singer can be accommodated in their studios, the owners of those studios invariably have ambivalent feelings toward their benefactor. Rick Hall withdrew his Fame label from Atlantic and placed it with Capitol in 1969, although he continued to produce Clarence Carter for Atlantic. The difference in sales between a hit by Clarence on Atlantic and by his wife Candi Staton on Capitol-distributed Fame, tells an important story.

While Clarence had a million-seller with "Patches" in 1970, Candi's hits were mainly confined to the R and B market, getting airplay on black-programmed radio and distribution to stores in black neighborhoods, but never "going pop."

Rick himself could see what was happening: "When Capitol sold two hundred and fifty thousand on Candi Staton's singles, they figured that was enough, that was as much as they could expect from an R and B record. But Atlantic would push theirs to a million, and then go for two million.

"I went to Capitol on my terms. They didn't have a promotion team, so I said they had to set one up, they had to hire twelve people to push their R and B product, which was all going to come from me and from Holland-Dozier-Holland [former Motown producers who had formed their own label, Invictus]. I went with Capitol because they gave me the advance I wanted. Atlantic wouldn't pay it."

Rick Hall is by reputation pushy, insensitive, self-important, and inconsiderate of his musicians. In person, he is much more aware of himself and others than that image suggests. He has a reason for his stern and apparently ungenerous treatment of writers and musicians, and an explanation for his refusal to distribute through Atlantic. He believes that his records would sell more copies through Atlantic's promotion and distribution system, but feels that Atlantic does not pay enough of an advance. And the only way he gauges his prestige in the music industry is by the size of the advance that a big company will pay for the honor of distributing his label.

Yet at the same time as he demands a high advance, Rick understands why Jerry Wexler refuses to pay it. "If I were in Jerry's position, I would not pay that much to distribute Fame. That's part of the problem between Jerry and me, we understand each other so well. He taught me how to operate, and now I've learned so well, he finds it tough to do business with me."

There's also a more particular cause of friction between the two men: Rick feels that Jerry encourages Rick's musicians to mutiny and desert. Jerry maintains that he is just offering help to unhappy musicians in their search for peace of mind. One of Rick's session groups who moved out on him set up a studio of their own a few miles away, called Muscle Shoals Sound. The nucleus of this group was Barry Beckett on keyboards, Jimmy Johnson on guitar, David Hood on bass, and Roger Hawkins on drums. Jimmy had been with Rick the longest, almost ten years by the time the move was made in 1969. "From 1960 to 1965 I played with a group called the Del Rays locally, traveling around the colleges, that kind of thing. And in late 1961 I got a job as a kind of all-around flunky to Rick Hall. He had a Concert tone tape recorder that had worn out, and he sold it to me for three hundred dollars. I didn't have that much, so I had to work for him to earn it, a dollar an hour for three hundred hours.

"I was working about four hours a day for about six months to get the money for that recorder, and it never did work, hasn't worked yet. But I didn't worry about that. I was his first secretary, I'd type out the contracts, he'd dictate letters to me."

When the original session band moved to Memphis, Jimmy became first choice for rhythm or lead guitar, and Roger Hawkins was the new drummer. But according to Roger, none of the musicians had much awareness of how their sound was registering in "the world outside" until Jerry Wexler came to the studio with Wilson Pickett in 1966. "Right away, Jerry started saying what a good band we had, good drummer, all of that, and nobody had ever said that to us before, that we were good."

In conversation, Roger and Jimmy confirmed and amplified what the Stax musicians had told Jann Wenner about Jerry's ability to develop a groove.

ROGER: Technically, Jerry doesn't know much about music. . . .

JIMMY: But he can feel a groove, and build it, so you feel it going right through your body. . . .

ROGER: I can be playing something on drums that doesn't seem anything special to me, but he'll say, that's good, and start getting other people to fit into it, till it *does* sound good.

JIMMY: When Jerry and Tommy Dowd first came down, we didn't know anything about things like fortissimo, and all that.

ROGER: But pretty soon we picked it up, double forte was *loud*.

JIMMY: One of the tricks of production they would have would be to do a blues song in a jazz key, you take a song from G to A flat and you've completely altered the harmonic structure, you've got it in a jazz key. Dowd and Jerry are very aware of the key the song is cut in, more so than the singer.

Later during the same conversation, the two musicians explained how they left Rick Hall.

JIMMY: We didn't want to be musicians for the rest of our lives. Just musicians. Which was all we had in store for us over there. We asked him if we could go into the company with him, and he decided he wanted to keep it all to himself.

ROGER: All we wanted was one percent, one percent each, of the profits.

JIMMY: Which we thought would have been a lot at the time, although now we realize it wouldn't have been much at all. But he said no, so we looked around for a way to get out on our own. We saw him getting ready to sign up the Capitol deal, which would shut out 90 percent of the Atlantic acts, which we had started out with. So we thought, if we start our own studio, maybe Atlantic'll keep using us. Which is what happened. So it didn't hurt Rick, because he kept getting stronger, but it led to Muscle Shoals getting even bigger.

ROGER: Rick's set in his ways, the way he cuts records. I think he could take any group of musicians and get a good sound from them.

JIMMY: He's on his fourth round now. We were his second,* and he lost the one after us, to Miami.

The group of session men Rick Hall lost to Miami was a collection of musicians pulled together by Jerry Wexler after he bought his winter home there. It seemed like the ideal setup for Jerry, and for a couple of years hits came from Aretha, Brook Benton, and others, produced by Jerry in conjunction with engineer Tom Dowd and arranger Arif Mardin. Everybody enjoyed the weather, but perhaps because the work wasn't regular enough, the session group dispersed, and subsequently Jerry called in people from around the country when he needed to cut a record in Miami.

The introduction of Arif Mardin as an arranger for R and B records was consistent with the tradition of Jerry's productions for Atlantic, which were very often more elaborate than other R and B records made at the time. In the late fifties and early sixties, Ray Ellis and Stanley Appelbaum had often provided charts for strings or vocal choruses, and now after a period when Memphis and Muscle Shoals records had been relatively uncluttered, Arif was asked to supply "sweetening." Trained as a classical

---

*In addition to his own regular groups, Rick also sometimes used Memphis musicians including Chips Moman and Tommy Cogbill who played on the Aretha Franklin date.

musician, Arif had been introduced to Atlantic by Nesuhi, who suggested he attend some jazz sessions and make any contributions he could think of. When Jerry saw how he worked, he began using Arif too, finding that here was an interpreter who could translate into musical notation the ideas for harmony lines and emphasis that he could not express musically himself. But musicians sometimes found it frustrating to work with the combination of Jerry, Arif, and Tom, particularly with singer-composers or singer-arrangers who could supply the musical framework for their songs themselves.

"It was very hard work, doing Atlantic sessions," one of the side men who played regularly on Aretha Franklin records recalled. "Take Aretha Franklin, for instance. She would run down one of her songs, and we would listen, and feel what each of us could contribute to it, on organ, bass, rhythm guitar, lead guitar, drums. We had been called to the session because we were known to be good, professional musicians, and we understood what could be done for the song. But the next time through, when we begin to join in, we're stopped. The arranger has an idea for breaking the tempo. Now we can feel where that would go, but he wants it two bars earlier. We're paid to play what we're told to play, so we do it, but we can feel it's wrong, and finally the arranger realizes what we knew in the first place, that the break has to be two bars later. Now that takes a long time, but we're not through yet, because after the arranger has said what he thinks has to happen, there are still more people who are there, who need to feel that they have contributed something to the record. It can take a week doing one song that way."

Arif and Tom Dowd worked with Jerry on virtually every Aretha session from 1968 onward, but in that period Jerry had considerably reduced his direct involvement in R and B sessions. Still indulging in the fun of building an

Below right: In 1970, Atlantic's promotion vice-president Henry Allen (centre) picked up rights to "Groove Me" by King Floyd, produced in the Malaco studio in Jackson, Mississippi by Elijah Walker (left) and Wardell Quezerque (right). A year later, Betty Wright (above right) launched the lighter Sound of Miami with "Clean Up Woman," with a classic guitar figure by Willie "Little Beaver" Hale. Two years later, Atlantic picked up "Soul Makossa," recorded in Paris by Manu Dibango of Cameroon (above). Despite minimal radio play, it became a top 40 hit in the summer of '73, highlighting the growing influence of dance clubs, now known as Discos.

R and B empire for Atlantic, he continued to sign up both established and promising talent, developing a roster which in 1971, for example, contributed nine of Atlantic's eleven million-selling 45s. But several of these R and B hits were records on small labels which Atlantic acquired for national distribution, and most of the others were independently produced. Although he does not talk about it, one of Jerry's biggest disappointments in Atlantic today must be the failure of the company to discover an effective R and B producer to take over from him. For a while, it seemed that he had found the answer in the team of Dave Crawford and Brad Shapiro, who came up with a few hits for a couple of years, but never quite hit the mark.

Crawford was a disc jockey in Atlanta who did occasional independent productions in his spare time. Jerry heard what he had done and recognized the sound. "They sounded exactly like my kind of record—they came out that way, even if he hadn't made them exactly as I would have done. And we're frail human beings, when you hear something that sounds the way you would have done it, you say, hey, that's my man. So Dave Crawford was my man, he was making my type of record. I asked him to come in as a house producer for Atlantic, and one of the first sessions he did was Jackie Moore's 'Precious Precious.'"

Actually, the official A side of the Jackie Moore release was "Willpower," but the record got no reaction and had been forgotten when a disc jockey flipped it and started getting requests for "Precious Precious." Atlantic repromoted the record with emphasis on the former B side, and eventually sold "one-eight" on it, music business shorthand for one million, eight hundred thousand. To Jerry's intense annoyance, *Billboard* never registered the record higher than number 30 in its Hot 100, insisting that it was only being bought by black record buyers whose purchases were registered in the Soul chart.

Not long after "Precious Precious," Jerry teamed Dave Crawford up with Brad Shapiro. Brad had been working for Henry Stone's Alston label in Miami, and Jerry felt that Atlantic could make more use of his talent. He chose to put Dave and Brad together "because a good team can be ten times as strong as one man, not just twice as strong. With one guy inside and one guy out, one in the studio and one in the control room, each of them acts as a sounding board for the other's ideas. They both have great song sense, Dave is a great song writer and Brad is a very good song sniffer. We've always worked in teams at Atlantic, first Herb and Ahmet, then Ahmet and me, and when Ahmet and I split up the work, I always worked with somebody, often Tom Dowd as engineer."

But although Brad and Dave produced a number of commercial-sounding records for Baby Washington, Dee Dee Warwick, and others, they mysteriously lacked the magic that makes hits, and Jerry has been obliged to send his R and B singers increasingly to outside producers, which means paying higher royalties. The Philadelphia team of Gamble and Huff worked effectively with both Archie Bell and the Drells and Wilson Pickett during the late sixties, while more recently Thom Bell produced a million-seller with his first record for the Spinners, signed from Motown by Atlantic. Muscle Shoals Sound also had a million-seller with Wilson Pickett, but the Malaco studios in Jackson, Mississippi, were disappointingly insensitive to the needs of New Orleans singers Johnny Adams and Irma Thomas.

Despite these setbacks, Jerry seems determined to maintain R and B as a major element of Atlantic's output, and was rewarded for his faith when a live album by the Chicago pianist-arranger-singer Donny Hathaway earned a Gold Record in 1972. Yet there was a period, around the time of the NATRA convention in Miami in 1969, when he must have seriously reconsidered his attitude to R and B music. NATRA stands for the National Association of

Radio and Television Announcers, a black broadcasters' organization that in 1969 named Atlantic as the record company that had contributed most to black music during the year. As unofficial head of the label's R and B department Jerry had been expected to go onto the platform to receive the award, but Henry Allen went on stage instead. According to rumor, Jerry was warned by phone in his hotel that it would be safer for everybody if he didn't show his white face on stage. Henry Allen is Atlantic's veteran R and B promotion man, the voice and the face that most black disc jockeys know best since Jerry retired from full-time promoting. According to the rumor, a powerful lobby within NATRA felt that since Atlantic was making so much money through its black artists, a black executive should receive the award. Although Jerry has not confirmed this rumor, there was certainly an undercurrent of terror and violence running through certain parts of the music business at that time, an undercurrent which emerged a few months after the conference in the gruesome murder of Harold Logan, long-time associate of singer Lloyd Price. Logan was found stabbed to death in his Broadway office, with the record player in the office fixed so that Lloyd's latest record played repeatedly.

Even if this did not diminish Jerry's enthusiasm for R and B, it was still true that he had achieved just about all a man could conceivably achieve for the music. He had identified and brought together some of the best musical talents in the country, and helped them to make records that were at the same time commercially successful and artistically satisfying. What else was there to do?

Well, there was country music, the sound of the white South. In a subdued, almost reverential voice, Jerry confesses that his favorite singers are not the black singers he has worked with for most of his career as a producer, but "country chicks." "I love country music. I find great songs there—I like Merle Haggard, Johnny Cash. Charlie Rich is probably my all-time favorite, Waylon Jennings, Jerry Lee Lewis, Dave Dudley. The big turn-on for me are the country chick singers, Dolly Parton, Tammy Wynette, Loretta Lynn, the stone country girls. We've never entered that field because we didn't have time to become specialists in it."

Actually, Atlantic did record Dottie West in the early sixties, but presumably failed to sell enough to make them feel like extending the experiment. "Bob Montgomery came to me one time, and said let me start a country and western department in Nashville for Atlantic, give me the budget and I'll do it. So I said fine, but I hemmed and hawed over it, nothing was done, and he went over to start one for United Artists, and had a great run, Bobby Goldsboro and all those."

SWAMP MUSIC

Unprepared to set up a whole department for country music, instead Jerry developed a stable of southern white singers and musicians who were closer to pop, rock, or R and B: Delaney and Bonnie, Sam Samudio, Ronnie Hawkins, Dr. John the Night Tripper, Jesse "Ed" Davis, Duane Allman. Meanwhile he admired and perhaps coveted Doug Sahm of the Sir Douglas Quintet, Taj Mahal, Joe South, and Tony Joe White, all contracted to other labels.

Jerry rejected and resisted most of the heavily electric music emanating from Britain and San Francisco. "The rock bible writers worship electrical energy. Me, I opt for music. They can have kilowatts and ohms and ergs, but I like Taj Mahal. Taj tracks are porous, wide open—there's

Delaney & Bonnie & Friends, whose musical hot pot of gospel, country, and blues led to a whole new genre of music that Jerry Wexler likes to call Swamp Music.

not that great dependence on electricity. To me, the biggest, most distinctive feature of rock is the sustained tones of the rhythm guitar, whether it's coming from reverb or fuzz box or echo chamber. The drone sound fills the spaces. Your master-typical rhythm guitar player is Chuck Berry—he's the master and he did not sustain all his tones, he didn't fill every gap in."

In an article for the special edition of *Billboard* that celebrated its seventy-fifth anniversary in December 1969, Jerry laid down his love for Southern music with generous disregard for who was not on his label and who had recently turned their backs on him.

What It Is–
Is Swamp Music–
Is What It Is

At drummer Sammy Creason's Halloween party in Memphis, his new boss, singer Tony Joe White, holds his breath to close his pores, removes a black widow from his personal mason jar of spiders and puts it on the back of his hand. The spider bites, the assemblage murmur their orison of Far Out's, somebody puts Tony Joe's new "Roosevelt & Ira Lee" record on the record player. Tony Joe courteously offers a spider to Stax producer Don Nix, discoverer and producer of Delaney and Bonnie. Don, who has been wearing Buffalo Bill hair and a Dennis Hopper Easy Rider getup for five years now and who has been roaming the southern hills and marshes and savannahs all these years in monomaniacal pursuit of some private musical vision, has no problem in passing the spider in favor of a roach.

At 3614 Jackson Highway in Muscle Shoals writer-guitarist-singer and embryonic guru Eddie Hinton works out a Taj Mahal rhythm with drummer Roger Hawkins and it is finally figured out the only way is to start the beat on two instead of one. The session is Ronnie Hawkins' first for Atlantic and the tune is "Who Do You Love" and although Ronnie has been owning a couple of farms outside of Toronto and a night club or two in Toronto, he is still stone Arkansas swamp and you'll never hear a bitter breath or a bad vibration from the guy who lost Rick, Rick, Levon, Garth and Robbie to Dylan and Fred Carter to the Nashville studios and John Till to Janis Joplin.

At the Ash Grove in LA, it's a Monday night jam with Taj on harp and noble Jesse Davis on guitar. Leon Russell sits in on piano and then Big Boy Crudup comes on to sing, and that, as Stanley Booth, the sweetest pop journalist south of the Smith & Wesson line says, makes some kind of a blues band.

At Ungaro's, 70th near Broadway, Dr. John extinguishes flambe headgear, waits for the goofer dust to settle and the gris gris to dry up a little and finally applies ass to piano stool. Delaney Bramlett, Eric Clapton and Ginger Baker sit in and they do things to "Tipitina" that could just possibly make you forget Professor Longhair, the marvelous valetudinarian architect of this New Orleans all-time 8-bar anthem. You could sing "Stack O Lee" to these changes, or "Ain't Nobody's Business," or "Cherry Red," but the way Dr. John (né Mac Rebennack) phrases it, it's got to be Longhair's swampy incantation that sounds like "moolah wallah da" and how the hell did we ever spell it on the lead sheet?

At another studio in Muscle Shoals, Rick Hall's Fame, Bobbie Gentry cuts her fantastic song, "Fancy," and Rick's new rhythm section burns in a beautiful track. Solomon Burke gets an advance copy of Tony Joe White's new album from Donnie Fritts, the elegant Alabama Leaning Man, and does a hell of a cover on Tony Joe's "The Migrant"—at 3614.

Two weeks later at the Criteria Studio in Miami, Brook Benton, with the promising new Florida rhythm section, Cold Grits, does Tony Joe White's "It's a Rainy Night in Georgia." The Pasha, Arif, is producing, and his Soulful Turkish Eminence gets a fantastic track from Tubby-Harry-Jimmy-

Billy with Cornell Dupree extra added on guitar
and Dave Crawford on piano.

Emergent Thing

In Memphis The MG's are still the top funk group
and Duck Dunn is running with Don Nix a lot,
and Chips Moman's guys at American are doing
tremendous things behind Elvis, Dusty, Herbie
Mann, and Dionne. Clapton has joined Delaney and
Bonnie. Leon Russell is in England cutting his LP
with Harrison and Clapton backing. Father Mose
Allison is carrying on in his spare, flame-
under-a-bushel style. Creedence Clearwater is taking the world. Aretha is cutting a Dr. John tune.
Pickett cuts another. Dusty did Tony Joe's "Willie
and Laura Mae." Doug Kershaw is making small
seismic waves and Clifton Chenier is getting
reviewed by Greil Marcus. Huey Meaux is back on
the stick.

What it all is is swamp music—is what it is.

That is what everybody is calling this emergent
thing which is just about here getting past our noses
and laying where you can get a look at it and say
"I Be Dog": Sure!! It is the Southern sound! R&B
played by Southern whites! It is up from Corpus
Christi, Thibodaux, Florence, Tupelo, Helena,
Tuscaloosa, Memphis! It is the flowering of the
new Southern life style! It is Duane Allman, the
Skydog guitar wizard out of Central Florida whose
hair is longer than Dennis Hopper's and who was
more shook after seeing "Easy Rider" than, at a
guess, Jack Newfield or Albert Goldman. It is Southern rhythm sections made up of young country
cats who began with Hawkshaw Hawkins and

turned left behind Ray Charles and Blue Bland.
It is Joe South and his great gift of melody and
the lowest-tuned guitar this side of Pop Staples.
It is the spirit of Willie Morris, born in the Delta,
schooled in Texas, and arrived on the literary scene
in New York as editor of Harper's at 32, and who
with Faulkner calls the black people of his home
his kin.

Country Funk

It's country funk. The Byrds put something in
it, Ray Charles added a lot. It's a pound of r&b,
and an ounce or three of country. The music has
Cajun swamp miasma, a touch of Longhair's New
Orleans blues rhumba, some of Taj's recreations
of Cow Cow Davenport's buck dance thing. It has
been shaped by Otis Redding's horn thinking, Steve
Cropper and Reggie Young's and Chips Moman's
fantastic section guitar work—part lead and part
rhythm on the same tune. It has Tommy Cogbill's
structured variations of the rhapsodic Motown bass
lines. It has Roger Hawkins' gut-stirring, beautiful
snare hit. Jim Stewart and Rick Hall and Chips
and Tom Dowd picked up where Sam Phillips left
off and poured it into Sam & Dave and Clarence
Carter. It's a lot of gospel changes and very, very
rarely 12-bar blues.

It's not rockabilly, either, but the echoes of early
Sun are there. Ghosts of beginning Elvis and Cash
and Vincent; listen to "Suspicious Mind" live with
the Sweets backing Elvis, and that's definitely it.

The words? They are plain old representational
words—Southern folk communicating with each

other in beautiful, unornate spare earth talk. There is field lore. There is love on a farm. There is swamp myth. The people who play it and sing it are conditioned by the way they grew up, Southern lifestyle: it's in the ground they walked on, the grits they ate, the water they drank. Their imagery has humor and insight, and the references, although they are regional and even parochial, are easily comprehended.

What it isn't: it isn't the private replay of a trauma that happened to a 12-year-old girl balladeer in her aunt's hayloft in Barnstable, Mass. The sounds aren't super-overdubbed. There is no use of feedback, 10-foot amplifiers, excessive reverb, no souped up treble.

What it is is authentically country Southern, and the exceptions, Taj, Fogarty and four of The Band don't disprove a rutting thing because they know what the roots are.

And it is also available for export: Listen to "Come Together" or "Midnight Rambler." The superb, fantastic "Abbey Road" has them kind of tracks, Cousin, and the magnificent Rolling Stones are a super rhythm section. "That's what we are," Mick says, "a rhythm section."

What else? Well, Sir Douglas, yes, and Johnny Cash and Merle Haggard; they surely fit into this swamp thing, and Jerry Lee Lewis today and the great, tragically, underrated Charlie Rich.

And Phil Walden is in it, in Macon where he and Otis began and from where he manages Duane and Tony Joe and Clarence Carter.

There's more—it's only just beginning.

Rhetoric and contradiction fill Jerry's piece, and surely bait does too; the head of a record company would be wise to call the last LP by the Beatles "superb, fantastic," and the Rolling Stones "magnificent," even if the relevance of those acts to a piece on southern music is tenuous. But still, that article is better written, more infectious, and more engaging than most current rock writers could manage. Just as he had done in his piece on "cat music" in 1954, Jerry pinned to the page a wave of change that emanated from several places in the world simultaneously, and which the outside world has taken three more years to assimilate and understand.

Of the southern artists contracted to Atlantic, by no means all of them were Jerry's "discoveries." Delaney Bramlett, Jesse "Ed" Davis, and Dr. John were all first encountered by Ahmet at Los Angeles sessions. But it was Jerry who took the musicians under his wing, who encouraged them to record in Miami, or who flew to attend their West Coast sessions and contribute suggestions.

The important difference between this new back-to-nature rock and R and B was that there was no ready-made audience for it. The Southern Groove of the Memphis and Muscle Shoals studios had evolved in recording studios and was disseminated to the world through radio, but this country gospel rock had to be introduced through live performances. The new music was launched in a succession of tours by Delaney and Bonnie and Friends (who sometimes included Eric Clapton and Leon Russell), by the Joe Cocker Revue under the banner Mad Dogs and Englishmen (including Russell), by Derek and the Dominoes (featuring Clapton), by Leon Russell himself, and by the Allman Brothers Band. At the same time, already established acts, principally the Rolling

Stones and Ike and Tina Turner, emphasized the sing-along possibilities of their repertoire (in the case of Ike and Tina, this involved introducing an almost complete-ly new repertoire), so that concerts came to resemble re-vivalist meetings.

In many ways, all these traveling road shows were repeating what Ray Charles had done with the Rae-lettes and band in the late fifties, when twenty-minute versions of "What'd I Say" and "I Got A Woman" would raise an audience to its feet. The increased media coverage now generated a feeling of bigger "events," which for some culminated in the 1971 Madison Square Garden Concert for Bangladesh, where George Harrison and Bob Dylan were backed up principally by musicians from the South, including Leon Russell and Jesse Davis, and by singers who had accompanied Percy Sledge on "When A Man Loves A Woman."

Whereas Atlantic had been clear ahead of the field in its involvement with the Southern Groove during the sixties, it is just one of several companies now involved in country gospel rock—a fusion of gospel, country, and rock 'n' roll that Jerry likes to call swamp music. A & M, conveniently headquartered in Hollywood, where the music was first developed by migrated southern musicians, Elektra, and Leon Russell's own Shelter label have as many important groups as Atlantic, while CBS and Warner Brothers have used the traditional big business technique of paying virtually any price for any available act. In com-mon with other forms of music which evolved during the late sixties, "swamp music" allows for only a minor role for the producer at recording sessions. The musicians either write or choose their own material, decide what key to play in, and when to stop.

But despite the musicians' enthusiasm for playing the gospel jams, and despite the appeal to live audiences, "swamp music" has not really broken through to the general public in the way that rock 'n' roll did, or in the way that R and B did in the sixties. Leon Russell's most recent LP was a bestseller, but Atlantic's Ronnie Hawkins and Sam Samudio (formerly Sam the Sham) sold poorly, Dr. John remains a cult figure whose records don't sell much more than 50,000 copies each, and Delaney and Bonnie have had only sporadic success. The music business was amused when CBS belatedly came in on this sound in 1971 by buying up Delaney and Bonnie's contract for an undisclosed but reportedly huge figure, only to have the act fall apart under their noses when the couple split up, both as a private relationship and a business partnership. "Hey look," Jerry is said to have remarked, "CBS just got two acts for the price of six." Could it be, Clive Davis at CBS might have wondered, that Ahmet and Jerry had premonitions that their duo would not stay together forever?

The only group on Atlantic who looked as if they would take a version of this sound to more than a few thousand people was the Allman Brothers Band, who played a slightly different kind of music, a combination of conventional fifties-styled city blues and "spacey" solos—southern jams, without the gospel chants. The group functioned primarily as a showcase for the extraordinary guitar playing of Duane Allman, who came to Jerry's attention through his work on Wilson Pickett's "Hey Jude," produced by Rick Hall at Muscle Shoals in November 1968 during a six-month spell by Duane as a regular session musician there. After using Duane himself on some sessions, including Aretha Franklin's "The Weight," Jerry became convinced that Duane should be in a regular

**The Allman Brothers Band, featuring guitarist
Duane Allman (third from left).**

group, and suggested to Phil Walden that Phil put together a band for Duane and start a label to put it on. Capricorn Records (Phil and Jerry were both born under the sign) was set up in Macon, Georgia, in the same office where Phil already had his publishing and management company, while Atlantic took care of promotion and distribution.

As so often before, the management of the distributed label found that working "under" Jerry was too claustrophobic and confining. For the Allman Brothers, the arrangement worked out fine. Duane proved to be an outstanding technician with an amazingly sensitive instinct for constructing long solos which never lost a sense of direction, and with his brother Gregg singing and playing organ,

Dicky Betts playing very good second lead, and a supple rhythm section, the band grew in two years into the most consistently exciting live group playing regularly in 1971. Their double LP, *Live At The Fillmore* was awarded a Gold Record in 1971 for earning more than a million dollars in sales. Then Duane was killed in a road accident, just as the group seemed poised for superstardom.

But Capricorn was never intended to be a one-act label, and conflict developed between Jerry and Phil and his partner Frank Fenter over the nature of the label's roster. Jerry wanted a southern label, while Phil and Frank wanted a label with a southern flavor. So there was less R and B on Capricorn than Jerry had hoped, and instead some rock groups with much less flair than the Allmans, and singer-song writers who could as easily have been on any other label. The final rift came when the distribution contract was to be renewed, Capricorn asked for an advance which Jerry thought unnecessarily high, and Capricorn signed up with Warner-Reprise.

Yet another of Jerry's favorite sons had rejected him, and it really did begin to look as if he had become a difficult man to work with. Was he undoing all the good work he had done for Atlantic during the sixties? How did Ahmet and Nesuhi feel when one good distribution deal after another seemed to fall away from Atlantic? By the end of 1972, Buddy Killen had moved his Dial label, including Joe Tex, from Atlantic to Mercury, who immediately had a huge hit; Wilson Pickett moved to RCA, with Dave Crawford as his producer, and there were even whispers that Aretha would return to CBS in mid-1973 when her Atlantic contract expired. Perhaps to escape old relationships, and to restimulate himself by entering an entirely new field, Jerry announced in October 1972 that Atlantic was to start a Nashville-based operation.

NASHVILLE, TENNESSEE

Jerry evidently felt that Atlantic had to make a formal announcement about entering the country field if the company were to present itself as a credible label for country singers or writers. And Jerry believed Atlantic needed country writers because they came up with the best material, songs that could be recorded again by R and B singers or by pop-angled singers if their own versions were too obviously "country" for the top 40 stations. In the past, Jerry had been able to "find" good songs for his artists just by listening to country music radio stations, but too many other producers were onto that trick for him to be able to keep ahead of them. He needed access to unrecorded songs, and this was a good way to get some.

Jerry chose to make his debut appearance in Nashville in the week of the Country Music Association's annual convention, in late October 1972. It meant a week of dinners with long speeches and poor food, but it was the most efficient way of seeing and being seen by the largest possible number of people in the shortest possible time. He appointed an assistant to take care of Atlantic's Nashville affairs, Rick Sanjek, the son of Jerry's long-time friend Russ. Previously an official in BMI's Nashville office, Rick had already set up one artist to open up Atlantic's country roster, Troy Seals.

The week in Nashville was intended to prospect the field, stake out a corner, see who might be interested. A small deputation accompanied Jerry from New York to Nashville: Dicky Kline of the New York promotion staff, Bob Rolontz of the publicity department, Mark Meyerson of the A and R staff, and John Fisher, head of the West Coast promotion staff and a country singer himself on the side. At any other music business convention, the Atlan-

In Britain, Dusty Springfield was regarded as a "pop" singer; Jerry Wexler recognised a great soul stylist, and produced an album in Memphis with Chips Moman's session team at American Studios. Dusty's touching delivery on "Breakfast In Bed" and "Son of a Preacher Man" proved Jerry's case.

tic party would have attracted attention and respect, if not awe, but here it was a curiosity, a minor sideshow at an event where Capitol, RCA, and Epic supplied endless drinks to any hanger-on who asked for one. Still, Nashville did not feel like a real music city. Although stores that sold shoes, clothes, or clocks donated window space for displaying album covers, there were almost no clubs with live music, and few musicians playing for the fun of it. As Bob Rolontz commented, "Nashville is a historical accident, there's nothing here to make it the music center of the South. Almost every singer and musician who makes a living here is from some other part of the South, from Texas, Louisiana, Kentucky. It just happened that the Grand Ol' Op'ry was here, rather than Memphis or Shreveport, and the industry built up around it."

The general attitude of Nashville toward Atlantic can't have been much improved by the double-edged reception Jerry got from some of the visitors to his table. Whatever he felt inside, Jerry maintained a benign beam, Edward G. Robinson at his most benevolent, even when Joe Johnson, owner of the West Coast-based Challenge label, delivered the definitive fawning welcome.

While Challenge had some hits in the fifties, including "Tequila" by the Champs, Joe Johnson survived during the sixties as manager of the moderately successful country singer Jerry Wallace. Recently, Jerry Wallace has had a couple of big country hits which use the novelty device of wah-wah guitar, not generally used in country music. So it was an expansive, confident Joe Johnson who suddenly adopted a tone of reverence when introduced to Jerry Wexler. "Oh, Mr. Wexler, this is such an honor, you've no idea. I've admired your records for as long as I can remember. And we're really honored here in Nashville that you've come down here to join us. Now of course I know that you're a great producer yourself, and you've got a great staff there in New York, and I'm just an ignorant red neck country boy, but if there's anything I can ever do for you, produce a session, anything, just you call me, and I'll be delighted to help in any way I can. It's been a pleasure meeting you, Mr. Wexler, and like I say, we're real proud to have you here."

It will be fascinating to see if Jerry can find in Nashville, or some other part of the South, a performer rooted in the traditions of country music who can reach the mass popular music audience, as Johnny Cash has done. There will be a lot of people smirking behind the back of their hands if he fails.

NINE:
THE UNDERGROUND
GOLD MINE

While Jerry Wexler devoted his energy to R and B and southern singers, gaining the reputation of a man who cared passionately about his music, Ahmet Ertegun inscrutably consolidated and expanded the rest of Atlantic's roster. His ear for music was still true, although it was open to more diverse and commercial forms than was Jerry's. And Ahmet was probably more capable than Jerry of recognizing the commercial possibilities of a performer whose music he didn't personally like, while on the other hand he seemed less likely to sign acts for sentimental reasons, liking them and yet sensing that they might not sell.

But if that description suggests a calculating businessman, it doesn't take into account Ahmet's apparently boundless appetite for the Good Life, his extended holidays in Latin America and Europe, his New York socializing, and his perpetual practical joking. Working in short bursts, trusting his intuitive judgements about a person or his music, Ahmet depended heavily on the efficiency of his office staff, and on the much more conservative life style of his brother Nesuhi, who worked more regular hours in the New York office. Even when Ahmet was apparently at work, he still played his jokes.

One time, as Jerry tells the story, Ahmet was up at Nolan's rehearsal hall, a studio on Broadway where Atlantic and other New York indies used to rehearse. While Ahmet was standing in the phone booth near the door, he saw George Goldner come in with a rabbi carrying a guitar, and "two mambo chicks, two Palladium-type chicks." Ahmet watched as they went down the hall to a rehearsal room.

Ahmet turned back to the phone booth, called the other number for Nolan's, and asked to speak to Mr. George Goldner. The call was put through to George, who answered, "This is Mr. Goldner, who's that?"

Ahmet improvised, "This is Aberfaccio from the union."

"Yeah, well what do you want?"

"Well I'm Aberfaccio, I've taken over as delegate for the musicians, and I'm checking up on you record guys. What are you doing at Nolan's?"

Goldner got upset. "Look, I've got friends over at 802, Aberfaccio."

"Yes, I know you *had* friends over there, Goldner, but that's why I'm here, to check on all that stuff, because those days are *over*. Did you file for rehearsal?"

Filing for rehearsal was a union rule, which nobody adhered to. "Nobody ever files for rehearsal, what is this?"

"Starting from now, you file for rehearsal."

"Well, we didn't come here to rehearse."

"Oh no, so what are you doing?"

"We just met down the street and we came in here to talk."

"You hired a rehearsal room to talk? Okay, well I'm coming over to take a look."

Ahmet put down the phone, and watched the door down the hall open as Goldner, the Rabbi with the guitar, and the two mambo chicks came tearing through the lobby. Ahmet stepped out of the booth. As Goldner came toward him he slowed down gradually until he stopped right in front of him. "Ahmet. . . . ."

LOS ANGELES, CALIFORNIA

One minute Ahmet was playing games on Broadway, and the next Atlantic was competing with the biggest companies in the record business. Some of this increase in turnover resulted from Jerry's maneuvers in the South, but even more came from Ahmet's advances into the pop field.

According to Jerry, "The whole pop thing for Atlantic came out of the "Splish Splash"/"Queen Of The Hop" session that Ahmet produced for Bobby Darin. Ahmet produced everything else that Bobby cut in New York, and when Bobby went out to the Coast in pursuit of a career in the movies, Ahmet went out there too, and started meeting all the session cats out there."

Those session cats rejuvenated Bobby Darin, whose later New York records had tended to be rather lifeless. A revamped "You Must Have Been A Beautiful Baby" came out of the first West Coast session and put him back in the top 10 in 1961, but better yet were the clever words and catchy arrangements of his own songs that followed: "Irresistible You," "Multiplication" and especially "Things." But once again, a successful artist was seduced away from Atlantic by a company with a bigger checkbook. Capitol signed Bobby up as "Things" became a big nation-

At right: Yet another At-
lantic artist leaves the
label at the height of his
success: Capitol boasts
their capture of Bobby
Darin. Below: Four years
later, Bobby is back. In
1966 pin-stripe suits were
the order of the day for the
well-dressed singer, as
well as for well-dressed
record executives.
From left to right:
Jerry, Nesuhi,
Bobby, Ahmet.

oh!
look
at me
now!

al hit, and had a couple more before Bobby tailed off. Four years later, Atlantic took Bobby back and squeezed one more top 10 hit out of him, "If I Were A Carpenter" (1966).

Ahmet doesn't talk much about how he sees his role as a producer, or what effect he has on the final product, but an engineer who recently worked with him was impressed particularly by Ahmet's ruthlessness. "He will spend a day with arrangers, trying all kinds of completely different treatments on one song. And as they begin to get discouraged and tired, Ahmet increases his enthusiasm, telling them that what they just did was fantastic, exactly what he wanted. Then at the end of the day when they've all gone home, he listens to the tape and says junk it. Next day we start again, with a new idea he has which works fine. But I was quite taken aback by the calculating way he flattered everybody into working so hard."

One of the musicians who played on Bobby Darin's West Coast sessions was Nino Tempo, who persuaded Ahmet to sign him and his sister April Stevens as a duo. Their "Deep Purple" was a national number 1 in 1963 and although the follow-ups tended to sound just like it, Ahmet found Sonny Bono at those sessions. The records Atlantic subsequently produced with Sonny and his wife Cher finally made it clear to the world that Atlantic was not just an independent rhythm and blues company with broader pretensions but an all-around company in fact.

Sonny Bono had been trying to make it since 1957, when he gave up his job as a delivery boy to assist in the office and studios of Specialty Records in Hollywood. Former New Orleans modern jazz musician Harold Battiste was manager on behalf of Specialty's boss, Art Rupe, at the time. When Harold was sent to manage a New Orleans outpost for the company, Sonny took over the West Coast office, producing, writing songs (for Larry Williams, Don and Dewey, and others), and administrating. But Specialty was on a downhill slide after earlier hits with Little Richard, and in 1962 Sonny set up his own company, Rush Records, which had no hits.

In 1963, Sonny met Cher and teamed up with her as a singing duo. The two reunited with Harold Battiste (now back in L.A.), who produced a couple of records that didn't sell. In 1964 Sonny and Harold evolved a plan which was one of the more ingenious hypes of the decade, more subtle than either the Monkees or the Partridge Family. Both Sonny and Harold had worked as session musicians on Phil Spector sessions, and had seen the legend of the producer-as-Napoleon spread through the media. So they planned to set Sonny up as a second Spector, with Cher as the equivalent of Spector's various girl groups. But where Spector and his artists were shadowy figures, Sonny and Cher would make themselves more visible, more easily identified. The only thing missing was a sound to focus on, and this was conveniently presented early in 1965 by the new phenomenon of folk-rock. Both Sonny and Cher could sing in the out-of-tune drone that Bob Dylan had adopted for his message songs; they applied the style to some of the nonpolitical songs in Dylan's repertoire, and to Sonny's own compositions.

Sonny did not bear comparison with Spector as a producer, which might have been a major problem, but Harold Battiste compensated for his weaknesses. Harold was an able composer and arranger who could provide the appropriate settings for Sonny's lyrics.

A one-off deal was made with Reprise for "Baby Don't Go," which flopped,* so Ahmet signed up the duo, at the same time as Cher was signed as a solo act for Imperial. This clever way of doubling advances was probably the

*Reprise reissued the record after Atlantic launched the pair, and had a hit in the wake of "I Got You Babe."

The shape and style of things to come. Sonny and Cher arrive in London, dressed to kill, with more records than they could count climbing both British and American charts. But the man who brought coherence to the sounds in Sonny's head, Harold Battiste (inset), was rarely seen. When Sonny ended his partnership with Harold, the stream of hits dried up.

idea of Sonny and Cher's managers, Charlie Greene and Brian Stone, but although it could have backfired by over-exposing the sound, in fact records by Sonny and Cher, and by Cher alone broke through together and were each followed by a succession of simultaneous hits. It had been an expensive risk for Ahmet, especially as the fees for the long sessions were huge, but it paid off. Greene and Stone hustled incredible publicity for Sonny and Cher, who were passed off as leaders of fashion and a perfect loving couple. Everything worked fine until Sonny came to believe his own image, figured he could do without Harold, and started producing alone. Jerry Wexler may have been taken in too, because he signed Cher and took her to record at Muscle Shoals Sound. "That kind of hurt," Harold recalled ruefully, "that they didn't make any approach to me, to say well we got Cher, and you were the one who found the sound to make hits with her, do you want to come and try again?" No hits came from Jerry's session.

Meanwhile, Ahmet had impressed Greene and Stone with what Atlantic could do for a pop act, and they came to him with some more. "Dynamite hustlers," according to Harold, Greene and Stone found a crafty way of drawing talent to their management agency. They moved into a vacant office at the Universal Pictures studio-office complex. So if a music act had any long-term ambitions to follow through into movies, surely here was a strategically placed agency to fulfill them. The UNI management didn't discover that they had squatters who weren't paying rent until Greene and Stone blew their own cover by asking the man who delivered pay packets how come they weren't getting any. By the time they were kicked out to find another base for their operations, they had built up an impressive roster of acts, and Atlantic benefited from having first choice. In Sonny and Cher, the Buffalo

Springfield, Iron Butterfly, and Dr. John, Atlantic covered all four corners of the sixties' pop/rock field: top 40, folk-rock, heavy rock, and eccentric.

The image of Dr. John the Night Tripper was in some ways as phony as Sonny and Cher's, and Harold Battiste was once again behind it. During his New Orleans residency as manager of the Specialty office and as joint owner of the cooperatively run AFO label, Harold had used material by a local young song writer, Mac Rebennack, and when Mac arrived in Los Angeles in 1964, Harold found work for him as a session guitarist and keyboards player. Like many other session men, Mac grew frustrated working for incompetent producers who couldn't hear when musicians were playing in different keys from each other, "and when I saw what Dylan and Sonny could do even when they couldn't sing, man I figured it was time for me to try something."

But even compared to Sonny's voice, Mac's was rough, and he had to concoct a context which would make it acceptable. Together with Harold, he evolved a character called Dr. John Creaux, a Louisiana voodoo man who chanted mysterious rhymes, cast spells, and wore weird clothes. A band consisting chiefly of expatriate New Orleans musicians played suitably bizarre music behind all this, and the potion was put out on an Atco LP called *Gris Gris*. Although neither that LP nor any of the follow-ups sold well, Atlantic's support for Dr. John confirmed that it was a company which cared for underground acts.

Ahmet did not have much personal contact with Dr. John, simply signing a contract with Greene and Stone, and paying the agreed advance, which quite likely was never recouped by sales. But Ahmet somehow heard the potential of Iron Butterfly. This group's second album, *In-A-Gadda-Da-Vida,* was one of the unaccountable phenomena of the late sixties, staying high in the bestselling album chart for over two years, despite little advance publicity and almost no press coverage. A lot of people liked to lose themselves in the steady, enveloping sound of the twenty-minute title track, which was one of the early examples of what came to be called heavy rock.

But while Dr. John and Iron Butterfly were principally business arrangements that Ahmet made and then stayed clear of, he did become personally involved in the careers of the performers who constituted the Buffalo Springfield, particularly the group's lead guitarists and chief writers Stephen Stills and Neil Young. By all accounts, both men were extremely temperamental, and although both were clearly very talented, it's unlikely that many other record company executives would have shown the patience and encouragement that Ahmet had through 1966 and 1967, as the group showed unprecedented disregard for deadlines, contracts, and money. The Buffalo Springfield did have one top 10 hit, "For What It's Worth," written by Steve Stills, sung by Richie Furay, and featuring some attractive "Los Angeles"-style guitar—free-floating, spaced-out. But follow-ups lacked that song's clear construction, and the albums weren't backed up by well-organized national tours.

Ahmet financed many hours of recording sessions, and did what he could to hold the group together. But Stills and Young found it so hard to get along, they sometimes put their guitar parts or vocal overdubs onto tracks at different times, so they wouldn't have to meet even in the studio. Personality conflicts were later to become part of the lore of rock music, but at that time they were kept as quiet as possible, and the Buffalo Springfield crumbled away, out of sight.

Evidently determined to get right away from the rest of the group, Neil Young signed a contract with Reprise as a solo artist, while Stills jammed in a studio with Al

Kooper (the results of which were issued on the CBS LP, *Supersession*), and at home with David Crosby, a recent dropout from the Byrds, and Graham "Willie" Nash of the British group, the Hollies. Ahmet kept supporting Stills, waiting for him to decide what to do, and when Stills chose to form a vocal harmony group with Crosby and Nash, Ahmet secured the release of Crosby from CBS and Nash from EMI. As part of the deal, Poco, a group formed by the Springfield's former lead vocalist Richie Furay, was assigned to Epic, a CBS label. In the past, jazz musicians habitually had jammed on each other's records, sometimes using pseudonyms when their labels tried to prevent them, but this was a new era for popular music, when contracts were no longer an absolute deterrent to stars from playing and singing on each other's records.

The new formation's first LP, *Crosby, Stills, and Nash,* is widely regarded as a classic folk-pop harmony record, a new advance in the genealogy which went from the Weavers, through the Kingston Trio, Peter Paul and Mary, and Simon and Garfunkel, to the Mamas and the Papas. The huge sales finally recouped the advances that Ahmet had been paying out for four years to keep Stills' nose above the water.

After forming Crosby, Stills, and Nash, Steve left Greene and Stone's management, and joined the recently formed agency run by David Geffen and Elliot Roberts. Within a couple of years, this agency had brought several outstanding contemporary acts under its wings, and in 1971 a new label was announced, Asylum Records, formed jointly by David Geffen and Atlantic. It was expected that Laura Nyro, writer of "Stoned Soul Picnic," "Wedding Bell Blues," and several other hits, would move to Asylum from CBS, but according to an item in the Hollywood *Reporter* she was persuaded to stay with CBS, who offered around four million dollars in advances. But Joni Mitchell jumped

At left: The Buffalo Springfield as well-dressed group, on- and off-duty, 1966. Only Steve Stills kept his tie on, and only Neil Young (far right in both pictures) never did. From left to right in upper photo: Dewey Martin, Richie Furay, Steven Stills, Jim Fielder, Neil Young. Above: Stills (right) and Young (left) back together again in a rare live appearance by Crosby (second left), Stills, Nash (second from right), and Young.

from Reprise to Asylum, Linda Ronstadt moved from Capitol, Jackson Browne joined the label, and the "original" Byrds came together again to make an album especially for it. Atlantic was distributor for the new label.

Encouraged by the good image that Asylum very quickly developed, Ahmet and Nesuhi made a similar deal with Artie Mogull for the Signpost label. Mogull made his reputation as a promotion/publicity-conscious record man, and his label was less rigorously selective and consistent than Asylum. But there were intriguing implications in one of the acts that was placed with Signpost, Danny O'Keefe, a singer-songwriter from Seattle. A particular favorite of Ahmet's, Danny had had an album on Atlantic's Cotillion label that sank without trace in 1971, yielding no hit singles, indifferent reviews, and no impetus to his career. Almost two years later Danny recorded another album, including a song that Atlantic's staff felt sure would be a hit single, "Good Time Charlie's Got The Blues." With the double motive of giving Signpost a strong launching record and ensuring intense promotional activity for the single, Ahmet placed the album with Mogull, and all concerned benefited when the evocative loner's lament, "Good Time Charlie," made *Billboard*'s top 10, ironically even getting some play on country stations at exactly the time that Jerry Wexler was leading Atlantic's official entry into the country music field. But nothing else on Signpost was as successful, and at the time of writing Artie Mogull is reportedly joining MCA.

Another West Coast label distributed by Atlantic had a less auspicious start. Clean Records, run by former scriptwriter Earl McGrath, had made almost no impact after nearly two years in existence. But still, it surely was no coincidence that Atlantic was using other labels both to attract the best known West Coast talent, and to promote the unknown. The pattern that had been begun with R and B labels in the South had evidently spread to other forms of music, in other parts of the country.

NEW YORK, NEW YORK

In contrast to its activity during the late sixties in the rest of the country, and even in Britain, Atlantic found relatively little of interest on its doorstep, in New York. Other labels found all kinds of interesting and/or commercial stuff, including Red Bird (with the Dixie Cups and Shangri Las), Kama Sutra (the Lovin' Spoonful), Buddah (all kinds of bubblegum), Verve (Tim Hardin, the Velvet Underground), and Kirschner (the Archies). But although Atlantic put out one LP by Tim Hardin before he had evolved his style, and belatedly picked up the Velvet Underground for one LP just before they broke up, the label found only two local acts who had much success, the Young Rascals and the Vanilla Fudge.

Ahmet signed the Rascals after word spread through the New York record business that a dynamite group was playing in a Long Island club. Several other producers were in the audience the night that Ahmet went out to hear them, including Phil Spector and Leiber and Stoller. Spector needed a replacement for the Righteous Brothers, who had just moved to Verve, and Leiber and Stoller needed a male group to balance out all the girl groups who were selling so well on their Red Bird label. There was a lot of friendly but intense in-fighting, and the Rascals fell for Ahmet's pitch.

"Good Lovin'," the Young Rascals' second record, topped the *Billboard* Hot 100 in 1966. So did "Groovin'" in 1967, and "People Got To Be Free" in 1968. Accomplished musicians, with two accurate and evocative singers in Eddie Brigati and Felix Cavaliere, the Rascals were an

The Rascals: Dino Danelli, Felix Cavaliere, Gene
Cornish, and Eddie Brigati. As the "Young Rascals,"
they made some of the tightest white rhythm and
blues records ever, supervised by Tom Dowd.
Changing their name to "The Rascals," they
metamorphosed their sound into elaborately arranged
ballads, to the delight of Atlantic's arranger Arif
Mardin, who gladly took over the production of their
records. "Ahead of their time" in their concepts, the
Rascals weren't around when mass taste finally
caught up with spaced-out R&B: they had moved
onto CBS and spaced-out vocal jazz, which nobody
could keep up with.

ideal hit-making unit in their first years of recording while they were still relying on a deep dance rhythm produced perfectly by Tom Dowd. But they started moving toward a more ethereal style in "Groovin'," and that sound was too soft for Tom, who left them in the hands of Arif Mardin from that record on. "If they hadn't left that earthy sound, there'd have never been a need for Steppenwolf, Three Dog Night, the Flaming Ember. The Rascals could do that better than anybody," Tom lamented after the group finally left Atlantic, still on good terms but unable to come up with a sound that could sell. Their move to CBS didn't help them either.

In 1967, George "Shadow" Morton, formerly an engineer and producer for Red Bird and the guiding hand behind the bizarre teen-drama records of the Shangri Las, brought the Vanilla Fudge to Atlantic. This time his gimmick was to record epic-psychedelic versions of recent pop hits. "You Keep Me Hangin' On" got some play and sold a few copies in the summer of 1967, and made the national top 10 when Atlantic reissued and repromoted it exactly a year later. But although the group made several albums and acquired a cult following, it inevitably broke up, and Carmen Appice and Tim Bogart first regrouped in Cactus, then joined Epic's Jeff Beck in Beck, Bogart, and Appice.

But despite the company's failure to exploit New York talent, Atlantic's bosses probably don't feel many regrets about lost opportunities. The Lovin' Spoonful would have been welcome if they'd known about the group, but most of the other hits coming out of the city were processed pop records that relied almost entirely on the producer's ingenuity, and hardly at all on the native talent of the singers and musicians. And although Atlantic's image became increasingly more diffuse and harder to define during the sixties, it continued to be true that the label

tended to go for what Jerry called "the long pull," putting
the energy of producers and promoters into acts which
might take time to establish their appeal, but would then
hang onto their audiences. The curious success of Roberta
Flack fully justified this policy.

Roberta is not a "New York" singer in the literal sense;
she made her reputation, as Ruth Brown did twenty years
earlier, in a night club in Washington, D.C., and drew
the attention of Atlantic's jazz department. Nesuhi was
nominally head of jazz, and took a lot of interest in Atlantic's
output, but his chief assistant Joel Dorn, a former jazz
disc jockey from Philadelphia, carried most of the responsibility for finding talent and producing the records. Joel
produced the first LP by Roberta, a classically trained
pianist with a voice that seemed infinitely adaptable,
capable of dealing with Spanish love songs, English folk
songs, new-wave R and B, even Leonard Cohen dirges.
First Take showed off everything she could do, and was
given royal treatment by Atlantic's promotion department,
at that time (1970) in the hands of Jerry Greenberg.

"We figured this was a good album," Jerry recalled, "but
it might have been ignored, because there were plenty
of good albums coming out all the time. So we decided
to invest a few thousand dollars, and organized big cocktail
lunches in ten big cities across the country. We'd invite
all the press and TV people to the lunches, and when
they'd finished eating, Roberta would play. They'd pick
up an album and go away again. Either they'd like her
or they wouldn't. We took a chance that she had what
it would take to impress them. It cost between seventy-five
and a hundred thousand dollars, and it worked, we got
a lot of coverage on her, right from the start."

But although *First Take* and two follow-up LPs all did
better than might have been expected for a classy, "serious"
singer, Roberta did not reach a mass audience until 1972,

The cool and calculating Roberta Flack, leader of Atlantic's assault on the wealthy, easy-listening audience.

after Clint Eastwood—who presumably didn't attend any of Atlantic's cocktail lunches—included "The First Time Ever I Saw Your Face" (a track on *First Take*) in the soundtrack of his film, *Play Misty for Me*. Answering requests for the song from people who had liked it in the film, a New Orleans disc jockey cut the five-minute LP track to a more convenient three-minute tape, and generated enough interest for Atlantic to put the thing out as a 45. It became the bestselling single of the year, and *First Take* belatedly "went gold."

Although Roberta Flack was the first Atlantic artist to achieve mass sales with a soft, jazz-tinged, "supper club" sound, Ahmet, Nesuhi, and Jerry had always enjoyed this music, and had been issuing albums by this kind of singer since the mid-fifties, persevering with Chris Connor, Bobby Short, and Mel Torme without ever getting any of them across to the vast "easy listening" market which constituted the largest proportion of the market for CBS, still the company with largest over-all sales. CBS had Andy Williams, Tony Bennett, Johnny Mathis, and Barbara Streisand all doing well in this field, and late in 1972 Atlantic launched an assault on it with Bette Midler, who was taken to be a combination of Streisand, Mae West, and Judy Garland. The last of the torch singers (the first of the flashlight crooners?), "The Divine Miss M" was a remarkably accurate expression of the abrasive side of Ahmet's soul, flashy, witty, challenging. Already beloved of New York's gay socialites, she was welcomed by jaded rock critics too. And the clever thing was that her repertoire was all-embracing, stretching from Bessie Smith through the Shangri Las to Atlantic's own country/folk writer John Prine. If things worked out right, the next five years lay open for her to devour the entire catalogue of pop music's history. And Ahmet, who produced some of the tracks on her first LP, would surely have fun choosing songs for the next one.

LONDON, ENGLAND

Although popular music is now apparently established as an international form of communication, with hits in almost any idiom stemming regularly from Britain, Jamaica, and Holland, and occasionally from other countries, this open situation is still less than ten years old and dates back to the first hits by the Beatles in the States at the end of 1963. Before that, hits in the States that were produced elsewhere were novelties, "freak" hits that almost never established a viable market for any particular performer. Among the few British-produced hits, most were from British Decca, which granted first option for U.S. licensing rights to London Records. The other big source of indigenous British material, EMI, had a similar first-option arrangement with American Capitol, but that produced almost no American hits before 1964.

Atlantic, like most other American independents at the time, licensed its own material to British Decca for release in Britain, but had no automatic rights to any British material. Most other independents in these circumstances ignored British-made product, but Ahmet was interested. He remembered his own youth, when he had become a fan of Louis Armstrong and Duke Ellington in Europe, only to discover that unlike his European schoolfriends, his American contemporaries had never heard of the great musicians. Although European taste in general might tend to lag behind American taste, there were often minorities who were ahead. And what they liked, maybe Americans could be turned on to.

Atlantic acquired American rights to the leading exponents of the three major British musical trends prior to the Beatles' "group sound," skiffle singer Lonnie Donegan, instrumentalists the Shadows, and dixieland jazz clarinetist Acker Bilk, in 1960–61. Donegan sang an assortment of folk songs to the accompaniment of a strummed rhythm from guitar, bass, and washboard or drums. But although Atlantic issued a number of 45s in the States, the label never had a hit, which must have been frustrating and perplexing, since Donegan had had a hit in 1956, when London took "Rock Island Line" from British Decca and made the top 10, and he had another one in 1961, after Atlantic finally gave up, when Dot took up the U.S. option on "Does Your Chewing Gum Lose Its Flavor?"

The Shadows were a four-man instrumental group who had twenty British top 20 hits in the years 1960–65, starting with "Apache," which Atlantic covered with an identical version by Jorgen Ingman, who made number 2 on the *Billboard* chart. Yet when Atlantic took up the option on the Shadows' own follow-ups, they never once cracked the top 100.

With Acker Bilk, however, Atlantic was luckier. Most of Acker's early records were of little interest to Americans, revivalist New Orleans jazz-styled sing-along chants, with bits of clarinet in the chorus. But in 1962 he recorded a theme tune for a TV program with a string orchestra, which when issued as a single, "Stranger On The Shore," was an international hit, topping the American chart. In the same year, Atlantic had another foreign-made instrumental hit, "Alley Cat" by the Danish pianist Bent Fabric, which was mysteriously voted R and B record of the year by the music business.

Apparently well-prepared to deal with overseas material, Atlantic surprisingly missed out on the first wave of British singing groups. Perhaps, understandably, they underestimated the likely appeal of the music, since it must have seemed that either in their catalogue or in their Southern Groove records they could supply product superior to the early hits by the Hollies, the Dave Clark Five, and

Herman's Hermits, even the Beatles, the Rolling Stones, and the Animals.

Apart from licensing a prehistoric Beatles record, "Ain't She Sweet," made in Germany for the local Polydor label, Atlantic didn't really get in on the British group phenomenon until 1966, and even then not everything worked out quite right. The Spencer Davis group was dropped after "Keep On Running" was no more than a regional hit in a couple of places, which enabled United Artists to sign the group up and have a couple of top 10 hits. And the Troggs were licensed from their management in Britain but U.S. Fontana claimed the rights to them too, so although "Wild Thing" topped the charts in 1966, it was available on both Atco and Fontana and the proceeds were split. Atlantic carried on the fight for the next record and then let the group go.

More productive agreements were reached with British Polydor, Robert Stigwood, and Chris Blackwell. Not long after British Polydor was set up by its German parent firm, Atlantic switched its U.K. licensing deal from Decca to Polydor, with a clause in contract guaranteeing that Atlantic would have first option for the States on any British acts signed to Polydor. Through that arrangement, Atlantic acquired Cream for America, who provided Atlantic with numerous hit 45s and LPs, in addition to establishing the company's credentials as a home for heavy rock. Cream comprised three former members of successful British groups who wanted to escape from the restrictions of either pop or purist blues, and the group's music was louder, longer, and more intense than anything yet heard, partly because the three musicians were sometimes literally competing with each other to be heard.

When Cream inevitably curdled, Atlantic held onto all three members, and while records featuring the bass player Jack Bruce and the drummer Ginger Baker had only minority appeal, Eric Clapton's albums under his own name and as Derek and the Dominoes sold very well, particularly the latter group's *Layla,* which enjoyed a second life when the title track became a belated hit 45 in 1972.

None of Polydor's other British acts were comparably successful for Atlantic, who "lost" John Mayall when Polydor formed an American arm and signed Mayall to U.S. Polydor, thereby bypassing the arrangement that Atlantic would get any British Polydor act.

Apart from Cream, Atlantic's other big British act in the late sixties was the Bee Gees, three brothers whose dirge harmonies sounded a lot like the Beatles. Appropriately enough, Beatles' manager Brian Epstein, on behalf of the agency he owned in partnership with Robert Stigwood, played demo acetates of the Bee Gees to Ahmet. Jerry Wexler also heard them and didn't like the sound at all, but Ahmet was enthusiastic. Atlantic signed up the Bee Gees and acquired its first consistently successful British pop group, who regularly got played on AM top 40 radio (in contrast to Cream and other rock groups who usually got played only on FM radio).

The breakup of Cream might have been more upsetting to Atlantic if the label had not been able to present an almost instant substitute in Led Zeppelin, whose guitarist Jimmy Page had been a member of the Yardbirds for a while after Eric Clapton had left to form Cream. Jimmy might have been on an Atlantic record five years earlier; he went to New York for a short time with Bert Berns, who had discovered him while producing some sessions for British Decca in London. Bert's wife Eileen recalls that Jimmy stayed for a while and that Bert wanted to use him on some Solomon Burke sessions. But no union or immigration papers had been arranged, so Jimmy went back to London.

Led Zeppelin was a natural progression from Cream,

Eric Clapton, whose "progressive blues" group, Cream, established Atlantic firmly in America's white youth "rock" market in the late sixties.

Led Zeppelin, the most successful heavy group of its time. Clockwise from top left: John Paul Jones, bass; John Bonham, drums; Jimmy Page, guitar; Robert Plant, vocals.

more disciplined and controlled, but also more intense, particularly in Robert Plant's shriek-singing. Although only Jimmy Page had any kind of reputation before the group was formed, the sound was immediately accepted, and every album was a huge seller.

Led Zeppelin actually was signed to American Atlantic, but in the hope of discovering British acts before they developed reputations and consequently became expensive to contract, Atlantic opened a British A and R department with the intention of signing local acts. Two groups were found, Dada and Yes, but although Yes became one of Atlantic's chief moneyearners, and Dada's vocalist Elkie Brooks may still fulfill the potential that drew attention to her, Atlantic did not expand this branch, apparently preferring to wait for other British companies to go through the teething troubles of pulling a first album together, and then paying the asking price if it sounded good.

The most regular source of licensed material for Atlantic has been Chris Blackwell of Island Records, who built up his company through the British sales of Jamaican music, and then branched into British rock music. Among the groups Atlantic took for America were Mott the Hoople, King Crimson, and Emerson Lake and Palmer, who sold poorly, quite well, and very well, in that order. When Chris announced his intention to launch Island Records in the States, it was assumed that he would place his label with Atlantic, but he chose Capitol, perhaps influenced by the fact that at the time Atlantic seemed to be selling as many records as one organization could reasonably handle, and might not need to push his as hard as would the struggling Capitol.

Currently, Atlantic's most successful British groups are Yes (from U.K. Atlantic), Emerson Lake and Palmer (from Island), Led Zeppelin (signed to U.S. Atlantic), and the

Rolling Stones (on their own label, distributed by Atlantic). The first three of these are all essentially in the same field, "progressive rock," although Yes rely much less than the other two on any kind of dramatic stage act, and depend instead on a studious approach to music, both from themselves and from their audience. In some ways, they might be said to be successors of Vanilla Fudge, but instead of extending familiar songs and turning them into frameworks for improvisation, Yes construct their own material out of fragments of music and vaguely meaningful lyrics. Emerson Lake and Palmer are more influenced by classical music, and go in for extravagant pyrotechnics on stage, assuming an audience that will sit still and listen—or be assaulted by sound—for long unbroken stretches of time. It's hard to imagine Ahmet sitting down to listen to a whole concert, or even one side of a record, by either Emerson Lake and Palmer or Yes. But he might enjoy

Yes: progressive rock at its most abstract and successful.

Distributed by Atlantic: the Rolling Stones.

the flash of Led Zeppelin, and he would certainly get a kick out of the Stones.

The Rolling Stones came to Atlantic late, after eight years with British Decca and American London. They announced their intention to form a label, and were bombarded with offers. There are no public details of their decision-making process, but it is likely that the highest bids would come from CBS, RCA, and Warner Brothers, with Capitol possibly close behind. Atlantic would be likely to keep their advance down to what they could expect to recoup in a fairly short time, hoping to compensate with a pitch that was aimed somewhere between Keith Richard's soul and Mick Jagger's sense of humor. If sentimentality would carry any weight, the fight for distribution was a simple one between Chess and Atlantic. In their early days, when they sang and recorded other people's songs, the Rolling Stones had drawn most of their repertoire from one of these two labels. They'd taken more songs from Chuck Berry—who recorded for Chess—than anyone else, and some from Muddy Waters, Bo Diddley, and Howlin' Wolf—all Chess artists, but all recordings from the fifties. Among more recent records which the Stones covered, the majority were on Atlantic, for while guitarist Keith Richard and the other musicians in the Stones were trying to emulate the instrumental sound of Chuck and Bo in particular, vocalist Mick Jagger was shooting for soul. Mick covered songs by Solomon Burke, Otis Redding, Don Covay, and the Drifters (all recorded for Atlantic labels) before eventually switching almost entirely to original material written in conjunction with Keith.

When the Stones came to choose a distributor in 1970, Chess was a much-changed company from the firm that had recorded Muddy Waters, Chuck, and Bo. The founder, Leonard Chess, had died, not long after selling his company to GRT, one of the two gaint tape manufacturers in the States. GRT moved the Chess offices from Chicago to New York, deleted most of the blues and rock 'n' roll from the catalogue, and attempted to push Chess into current R and B in association with another GRT-distributed label, Janus. The Stones could not have been happy with what they found, but did get on with one man there, Leonard's son Marshall, a fan of theirs and somebody their own age.

Atlantic was apparently a complete contrast, still managed by one of the two co-founders, still committed to some of the music that had built the company up. And Ahmet had little of the pretentiousness, stuffiness, or phony heartiness that tended to ooze off some other record company bosses. On top of that, Atlantic had proved itself to be as good at marketing, promoting, and distributing as any other label. The Stones appointed Atlantic as their label's distributor, and gave Marshall Chess the job of label manager, coordinating their releases, scouting for new talent, standing in between the artist and the corporation in any flare-ups.

At the same time as it measured and contributed to the prestige of Atlantic, the distribution deal with Rolling Stones Records also indicated that the label was no longer the do-it-yourself company that its own publicity tended to imply. The management apparently accepted as an inevitable fact of business that although Atlantic had grown big through the efforts of its own producers and their ability to hear potential in independent labels, in order to stay at the top the company needed to acquire product which had more or less guaranteed sales, assuming good marketing and distribution. The Rolling Stones label would have such product, and so had the Woodstock Festival, a year earlier.

One of the major impulses for buying records is to have a souvenir of a live (or even televised) performance, so when New York attorney Paul Marshall offered Atlantic the recording rights to a forthcoming festival in upstate New York, Ahmet grabbed the chance. Before the event, it was not obvious how big or successful Woodstock would be. The three acknowledged leaders of the "new" music, Dylan, the Beatles, and the Rolling Stones, were not on the bill, but a remarkably high proportion of the other major rock acts were there. R and B acts were conspicuously absent, with no Motown performers, nobody from Stax, and none of Atlantic's black singers, not even Aretha Franklin. Atlantic, in fact, had only one act on the bill, Crosby, Stills, Nash, and Young, and in order to present even a significant proportion of the groups who played, Ahmet, Jerry, and Atlantic's attorneys had to do some tough negotiating. CBS president Clive Davis in particular was unwilling to allow Santana and Sly and the Family Stone to appear on another label, and in cases like that Atlantic had to suggest to the artist's management that it would be unfortunate if so-and-so did not appear on this documentary of the event. The artist's management then put pressure on the record company to see the light. In the end, almost everybody did—except The Band, Creedence Clearwater, and Janis Joplin, whose managements refused permission.

With coups like the *Woodstock* LP and the Rolling Stones label notched on his belt, Ahmet Ertegun seemed to be in a good position to celebrate his label's twenty-fifth birthday party in 1973 in grand style. And no doubt he would. But the record industry is not like most others; it is dealing all the time with a public that can never be relied upon, and a commodity that is subject to constant change. The market as a whole can be depended on, people will buy records tomorrow. But nobody can ever be sure which ones will be bought, and to stay at the top a record company must be very sensitive to fluctuations of taste. Even the deal for the Rolling Stones may not have been the sure-fire guarantee of profits all around that it seemed. In two years Rolling Stones Records came up with only two albums by the Stones themselves, *Sticky Fingers* and *Exile On Main Street.* Apart from them, there was a record featuring Moroccan Pipes, and a budget-priced jam session featuring some of the Stones and pianist Nicky Hopkins. Atlantic needed more releases than that to recover its advances and guarantees, and even the Stones themselves did not have the selling power that all the publicity might have suggested. *Exile On Main Street* was listed as low as number 31 in *Billboard*'s list of bestselling albums in 1972, despite having one of the most heavily reported concert tours in recent pop history. Among the records above them in the list was a collection on London of their 45 hits called, *Hot Rocks,* a double album by the Allman Brothers, *Eat A Peach,* and even a couple of other records on Atlantic by much less famous artists, a live album by pianist-singer Donny Hathaway, and an album of monologues by comedian George Carlin.

It seemed hardly possible, but as Atlantic moves into 1973, it treads with a wary step. Too many wrong expensive moves, and there could be trouble.

TEN:
THE YOUNG TURKS

In 1972, Atlantic made more money than ever before, which must have made Ahmet Ertegun, his brother Nesuhi, and Jerry Wexler very proud. But were they contented, happy, comfortable? Was Atlantic in 1972 what they had hoped for? Naturally, they could not say no to such questions, yet it seems unlikely that they would say yes to themselves. For by 1972 the company had become unwieldy, inflexible, too close for comfort to a "major."

Before I began researching this book, I expected to find that a major disruptive influence on the company would have come from the takeovers which affected its ownership during the sixties. But although those takeovers may have been temporarily unsettling, they probably had less long-term effect on the company than the natural organic growth, which would have happened anyway, and which resulted in an ever increasing administrative staff.

According to Jerry, the takeovers resulted partly from his own insecurity. Tomorrow never looked too promising, and so an offer of a secure income today was always tempting. In 1964, Atlantic's principal stockholders (Ahmet, Jerry, and Nesuhi) sold the company's publishing catalogue to Hill and Range. Jerry says the reason was that "we had been working hard all those years and never really saw the returns for it; most of the money that the firm was making went back into the business, and we couldn't short-circuit that without doing damage. We couldn't raise what we were paying ourselves, so we looked around for something we could get some money for, and the publishing catalogue was the best answer."

Atlantic lost a lot of valuable copyrights that way, songs like "Shake, Rattle, and Roll," "Money Honey" and "Since I Lost My Baby," which have become standards and will earn money regularly for years to come, but since then an even bigger backlog of songs has been built up in the company's Cotillion catalogue.

Through 1965 and 1966, Atlantic continued to flourish, but its owners still felt a nagging worry that the run of good luck could come to a halt any day, leaving them with nothing but a scrapbook and a warehouse full of unsold and unwanted records. But while they realized that the record company was a rather unreliable business to rely on for a retirement pension, they didn't want to extend Atlantic's business sideways into more secure but less creative "hardware" lines like phonographs and cassette recorders, and they didn't have enough spare cash to make significant investments in more stable businesses run by other people. The answer to their worries came in 1967 with an offer from Warner Brothers to buy up Atlantic stock in exchange for generous amounts of Warner Brothers stock plus a regular, high salary to each of the senior Atlantic executives.

This sale brought Atlantic into a relationship with Warner-Reprise Records under the umbrella ownership of Warner Seven Arts, but there was not much interchange between the two record companies until 1969, when the entire Warner Brothers operation was bought up by the Kinney Corporation. Kinney had its origins in car lots and funeral parlors, before emerging as a media conglomerate. But whereas Atlantic's directors had *chosen* to sell their firm to Warner Brothers, they had little choice when Kinney came in to buy up their parent organization— although Jerry pointed out that if he, Ahmet, and Nesuhi had threatened to resign, Kinney might have had second thoughts.

Under Kinney, Warners and Atlantic came together on a few large-scale decisions. They recommended that Kinney buy up Elektra, and proceeded to set up distribution branches in each major region of the States, thereby severing their ties with the independent distributors who had acted for them previously. On a smaller scale, all three companies continued to compete with each other, particularly in bidding for acts, but by setting up joint distribution they became, as a unit, a major company.

But Atlantic still differs from other major companies in one way. It has always supported itself, paying its advances out of its previous earnings, paying its staff out of its current income. This contrasts particularly with CBS, whose president Clive Davis has announced several contracts involving more than one million dollars in the past twelve months, contracts which could be financed out of the coffers of the multiinterest CBS organization if record sales do not meet his needs. So although Atlantic's references to itself as still "independent" are largely rhetorical, that element of justification remains.

But an accurate definition of Atlantic's status as a major or an independent is less important than the effects of its growth on its internal decision-making process. When Atlantic had an office staff of less than twenty people, it was possible for all of them to feel part of any decision that was made, to suggest modifications of it, to feel responsible for putting it into effect. But as that staff multiplied, Atlantic's three bosses generated underneath them an interlocking structure of three pyramids, near the top of which were understudies to Ahmet, Nesuhi, and Jerry, who took on many of the duties of running the company but few of the major decisions, and consequently little of the satisfaction.

It is impossible for me to identify and describe the exact nature of whatever dissensions exist within Atlantic's New York office. I spent less than a week talking to the staff and watching records being made in the studio, being mastered in the editing rooms, being scheduled for release, being pushed into envelopes with a scribbled message—IT'S A SMASH! Compared to any other bureaucratic office I had ever seen, this one seemed lively and efficient, the good-natured tone of bantering conversations broken only by impatient shouts and commands from Jerry Greenberg, who controls the day-to-day affairs of Atlantic and reports directly to Ahmet. Proud to have been a drummer in a pickup band as a kid, Greenberg made his mark in the record business as a promotion man for a New Haven distributor, where Jerry Wexler noticed his energetic, enthusiastic, and effective work for R and B records and hired him as his own assistant at Atlantic.

Alongside or slightly below Jerry Greenberg in the hierarchy of the New York office are several others who are about the same age, just past 30, including Jim Delehant (formerly editor of *Hit Parade*) and Mark Meyerson (son of Harry, ex-A and R man for Decca and MGM) on the A and R staff, and Dick Kline (previously an ace promo man for London Records) in promotion. These men constitute the vanguard of the new generation at Atlantic, all of them in the record business because of a passion for music, all of them deeply loyal to Atlantic and its tradition as a stronghold of R and B. Yet while each of them speaks warmly of Jerry, Ahmet, and Nesuhi, who in turn hold their deputies in high regard, there is an indefinable sense that the balance of effort, responsibility, and reward is not quite right. The case of Shel Kagan partly illuminates the problem.

Shel was working at Atlantic when I visited the office, with a special role in the A and R department to look out for the campus market. Watching "All in the Family"

Previously a minor group in Berry Gordy's Detroit-based Motown stable, the Spinners became Atlantic's last great soul act, delivering several major hits written by their Philadelphia-based producer Thom Bell and his partner Linda Creed.

on TV one night, he thought of recording some of the choice dialogue from the show, got the support of both Atlantic and the cast, and spliced together an album. A new departure for Atlantic, the album sold very well, but as a staff employee Shel was not on any kind of royalty or commission. When he asked for one he was offered a bonus, which he turned down, resigning from the company to go freelance, putting together an LP for RCA from the "Sanford and Son" show. When the time came for a second volume of "All in the Family," Atlantic was obliged to employ Shel to produce it, and to pay him a percentage on sales. But neither LP sold well and Shel was soon looking for a staff job with a record company.

There is no evidence that the current staff of Atlantic are all itching to be put on personal royalties, but it is a sign that the firm has become rather too large and impersonal when such thoughts begin to nag the creative staff. Only recently did it become possible for the young A and R staff to sign up some acts without having to consult the chief executives. If that becomes general practice, the company may have built into itself a way for more people to feel committed to Atlantic's product, but at the same time it could accelerate feelings of detachment from that product in Ahmet and Jerry. For although each of them enjoys the kicks of Gold Records and the other outward signs of success in the music industry, they both care more to be personally involved in music. Nesuhi, by contrast, gives the impression of genuinely enjoying the delicate diplomacies involved in managing a bureaucracy staffed with creative people.

A curious solution to these conflicts suggests itself: that Ahmet and Jerry might each retire from his position as executive vice-president of Atlantic, leaving Nesuhi in sole control, to rationalize the three pyramids into one.

Freed of the responsibility of financial affairs, and finally separated from each other, Jerry and Ahmet could each form independent, intimate record companies on the scale of Capricorn or Asylum. (Jerry could call his label Root Records, and buy from Atlantic the contracts of Dr. John, Doug Sahm, and Willie Nelson; Ahmet could name his Nuggie, reviving the pseudonym he sometimes used on his compositions, and reclaim Danny O'Keefe from Signpost.) Both labels could be distributed through Atlantic, although it would be interesting to see if both men would choose to attach themselves to the company.

I don't suppose Ahmet and Jerry will do anything remotely like that. Still, researching and writing this book has whetted my appetite for their way of life. I'm in the process of starting a record label myself.

ACKNOWLEDGMENTS

For giving me their hospitality and so much of their time, I'm indebted to Jerry and Shirley Wexler. Jerry doesn't know it, but he provided the inspiration, encouragement, and support which helped me to finish the book. Mark Meyerson in Atlantic's New York office, and Janet Martin in the London office, were very helpful when needed, which was quite often.

For being so true to the tradition of southern hospitality, I'm grateful to Phil Walden, Frank Fenter, Zelma Redding, and the staff of Capricorn Records in Macon, Georgia; to Al Bell and Donna Breakstone at Stax in Memphis, Tennessee; to Rick Hall at Fame in Florence, Alabama; and to Jimmy Johnson, Roger Hawkins, and Alan Walden at Muscle Shoals Sound, Muscle Shoals, Alabama.

For breaking their busy schedules to find time to talk, appreciative thanks go to the following: Herb Abramson,

Harold Battiste, Joe Bihari, Honi Coles, Morty Craft, Jim Delehant, Tom Dowd, Ahmet Ertegun, Nesuhi Ertegun, Hunter Hancock, Ben E. King, Bob Koester, Jerry Leiber, the Magnificent Montagu, Huey Meaux, Mac Rebennack, Bobby Robinson, Lelan Rogers, Kal Rudman, Russ Sanjeck, Al Sears, Seymour Stein, Mike Stoller, Jesse Stone, Hy Weiss.

For spending so much time digging into their archives for records and clippings, humble thanks to the following: in the United States, Pete Grendysa of Milwaukee, editor and publisher of *Nuggie,* a newsheet devoted to the first ten years of Atlantic's existence; John King of Memphis; and Pete Lowry of New Jersey; in England, Mike Leadbitter, tender guardian of the world's rhythm and blues; Bill Millar, author of *The Drifters*; and Johnny Swan. They did what they could to reduce my ignorance.

For pulling a chaotic manuscript into shape, applause to my editor, Paul De Angelis.

It's too late to thank King Curtis and Clyde McPhatter, who died while the book was being written, but *Making Tracks* is for all those who knew and loved them and their music.

Charlie Gillett, London, January 1973

REFERENCES AND
FURTHER READING

John Grissim. *Country Music: White Man's Blues.* New York: Paperback Library. So far, much the best book on contemporary country music, this includes a number of entertaining and illuminating interviews, notably with Shelby Singleton and Norbert Putnam, whose comments are relevant to this book.

Peter Guralnick. *Feel Like Going Home.* New York: Outerbridge & Dienstfrey, 1971. The chapter on Chess Records is one of the few attempts so far to identify the character of a record company. In addition, there's a moving chapter on one of Jerry Wexler's favorite singers, Charlie Rich.

Jerry Hopkins. *The Rock Story.* New York: Signet, 1970. The last chapter explains the breakup of the Buffalo Springfield.

Mike Leadbitter. *From the Bayou.* Bexhill-on-Sea, Sussex, England: Blues Unlimited, 1970. The complete story of

Goldband Records, a small independent label owned by Eddie Shuler in Lake Charles, Louisiana.

Peter McCabe and Robert Schonfield. *Apple to the Core.* New York: Pocket Books, 1972. A rare behind-the-scenes investigation into the record business.

Various authors. *The Rolling Stone Interviews.* New York: Paperback Library, 1971. Apart from Jann Wenner's interview with the M.G.s in Memphis, there are various references and allusions to record companies and their owners, particularly from Phil Spector, who talks about Ahmet, Jerry, and Atlantic.

Joel Whitburn. *Record Research, 1955-71.* Menomonee Falls, Wisconsin, 1972. The definitive pop music reference book, this lists every record that entered *Billboard*'s Hot 100 from the inauguration of the chart in 1955, correlated alphabetically by artist name.

Joel Whitburn. *Rhythm & Blues.* Menomonee Falls, Wisconsin, 1973. A parallel publication to *Record Research,* drawn from *Billboard*'s weekly surveys of rhythm and blues hits.

No entries have been made below for Jerry Wexler, Ahmet Ertegun, or Atlantic. Italicized page numbers refer to photographs.

PICTURE CREDITS

Photographs are reproduced courtesy of the following:

Atlantic Records: pages 6, 24, 36, 56, 57, 61, 87, 97, 100–101, 105, 114, 115, 130, 157, 159, 173, 176, 184, 187, 191, 206 (right), 210, 222, 223, 228, 246, 249, 254, 255, 258, 260, 267, 268, 270, 271, 281

Harold Battiste: page 249 (inset)

Billboard: pages 108 (bottom), 206 (left), 214

Capricorn Records: page 237

Cash Box: pages 92, 164

Tom Dowd: page 108 (top)

Chris Goddard: page 63

Tom Hanley: page 79

Phonogram Records: pages 122, 240

Record Mirror: page 161

Stax Records: pages 179, 187 (inset), 195, 203

Mike Stoller: page 146